DEVELOPING A 21st-CENTURY MIND

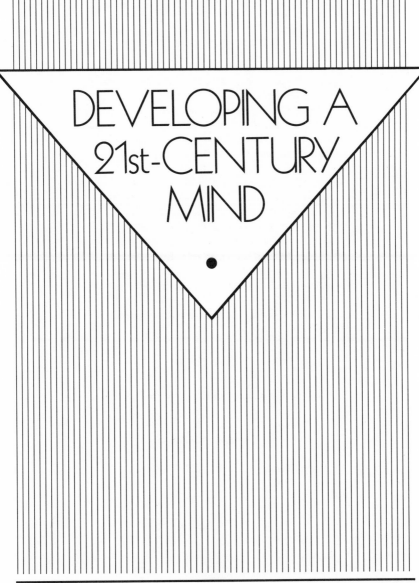

·MARSHA SINETAR·

DEVELOPING A 21st-CENTURY MIND

· Villard Books   New York 1991 ·

Comments and case illustrations are composites drawn from the profiles of hundreds of letters, conversations and interviews. None of these is meant to represent any one individual.

Neither publisher nor author assumes any liability for the use or misuse of techniques described in this book; nothing in this book is intended as a substitute method for competent therapy or professional attention.

Grateful acknowledgment is made to Liveright Publishing Corporation and Grafton Books for permission to reprint excerpts from "let it go—the" from *Complete Poems, 1913–1962* by E.E. Cummings. Copyright 1923, 1925, 1931, 1935, 1938, 1939, 1940, 1944, 1945, 1946, 1947, 1948, 1949, 1950, 1951, 1952, 1953, 1954, © 1955, 1956, 1957, 1958, 1959, 1960, 1961, 1962 by the Trustees for the E.E. Cummings Trust. Copyright © 1961, 1963, 1968 by Marion Morehouse Cummings. Reprinted by permission of Liveright Publishing Corporation and Grafton Books, a division of HarperCollins Publishers Ltd.

Library of Congress Cataloging-in-Publication Data

Sinetar, Marsha.
Developing a 21st-century mind / by Marsha Sinetar.
    p.   cm.
ISBN 0-679-40105-9
1. Self-actualization (Psychology) 2. Adaptability (Psychology)
3. Problem solving. I. Title. II. Title: Developing a twenty-first century mind.
BF637.S4S557   1991   90-45848
158—dc20

9 8 7 6 5 4 3 2
First Edition

Typography and binding design by
Marsha Cohen/Parallelogram

*I lovingly dedicate this book
to the memory of
Adele Sinetar.*

ACKNOWLEDGMENTS

My thanks to many people for professional support throughout the several stages of this work. Joan LaFlamme lent her editorial expertise when I first conceptualized this book. During countless revisions and manuscript alterations, editors (and my friends) Lynn DelliQuadri and Jill Hannum provided valuable organizing and manicuring input. Vice president and executive editor of Villard Books Diane Reverand greatly improved the readability of the final draft by encouraging additional cuts. Each of these clarified what could be a highly abstract technique. For all remaining flaws I fault only myself. For calm, steady patience during a lengthy writing period, I thank Linda Allen, my agent. Several exceptional individuals granted me interviews and sent me letters describing their creative process. To all, I express appreciation. However, it is to Pam Bacci, longtime friend and assistant, that special applause and acknowledgment are due, since she resumed her word processing on this book only days after the birth of her first child. This surely is what it means to go the extra mile, and I am grateful.

CONTENTS

DEVELOPING A 21st-CENTURY MIND

•

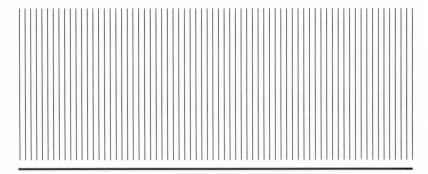

INTRODUCTION: UNITIVE INFLUENCES

For we know in part, and we prophecy in part, but when the perfect comes, the partial will be done away. . . . When I was a child, I used to speak as a child, think as a child, reason as a child; when I became [mature] I did away with childish things.

1 CORINTHIANS 13:10–12

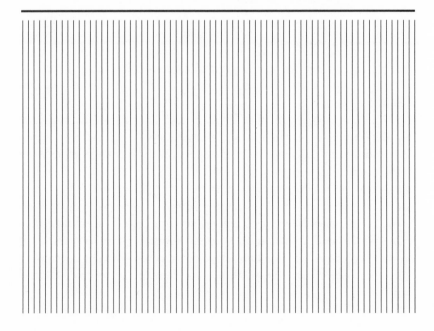

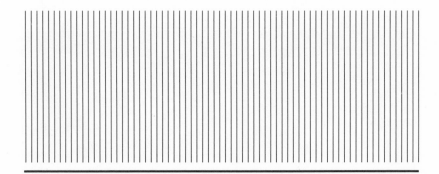

This is a book for people who feel themselves moving toward mature wholeness. The move demands the relinquishing of child*ish* things, yet paradoxically asks for a renewal of child*like*ness. Only the immature aggressively cling to fixity, overcontrol or the wish for guarantees. Faith, good humor, trust of the unknown are hallmarks of wholeness, and in this book I describe a playful path to developing what I call a 21st-century mind. To me, this is the mind of integration and full, creative health: although this mind sheds light on our best options and solutions, we rarely hear of it.

Almost everything we read and hear presupposes childishness, dependency, weakness, unproductivity. Today, neurosis, lovelessness, joylessness and addiction are considered "normal." Vigorous good health is a distant, largely idealized goal. Yet in keeping with a Buddhist notion, I believe that when people reach their highest perfection, it is nothing special—this is their normal condition. So, as I write of full personhood or mature wholeness and creative adaptation, I refer to ordinary people who are simply bringing their highest truths and values into daily life.

Millions of people are increasingly perceiving this normality, viewing self and other as synergistically interrelated. Such people long to love and work productively. They report themselves engaged in what I can only call a spirited dance. Millions more want to grow in this way—want to see the world connected and whole and safe. They yearn for liberation from the constraining, punitive, polarizing ideas and images of the past. Recent political events throughout the world reflect this wish beyond a shadow of a doubt. Grass-roots wholeness, even spirituality, is on the rise, and I hope that people who are developing into whole-seers will enjoy and benefit from my concept of *Positive Structuring.*

Positive Structuring is a novel consciousness-raising technique and process that offers psychologically healthy, mature adults a tool to "play" with, to guide and develop their own creative problem-solving skill. Positive Structuring suggests a way of perceiving that sees "the perfect" and does away with partial things. This is, in fact, what the word *wholeness* means. Since hard-to-solve problems are on the rise and since the future, for all of us, is uncertain, globally we must look for ways to strengthen creative thinking. I suggest links between very probable future scenarios and very practical implications of enhancing the processes of our own minds. As we strengthen and illuminate what is best within our hearts and spirits, urgent if unusual answers come. Each chapter briefly outlines such links, since I'm describing a technique for cultivating a higher thought process, not specifically drawing a picture about the future. Despite my focus, none can afford to ignore the transitional upheavals that lie ahead, and therefore I mention some of these, with particular regard to work and economics.

Our world is already characterized by constant, major, simultaneous change. Changes envelop and touch us all. Creative problem solving is the prerequisite skill for successful 21st-century living, since resourceful minds ably handle paradox, the unknown and abstraction. Chapter 1 discusses the creative mind and reviews some of the key behavioral outcomes of what I term *creative adaptation*. This is my phrase for the psychology of "personal entrepreneuring" or "overcoming": it is a term I use to describe people who artfully meet the unknown, crisis or rapid change. Throughout this book, I use the concept of creative adaptation as a vehicle to describe varying facets of the method I call Positive Structuring. Creative adaptives do more than merely adjust blandly to convention or tradition; when necessary, they successfully bend what exists to their life-purposes. Their minds are able, alert and inventive, and they receive no small amount of pleasure from their own creative processes and products.

At some point, creative adaptives discover that, instead of their continually submitting to the world, the world has adapted to them—even if only in part and over the long haul of their lives. To lean on Joseph Campbell's inspiring phrase, they "follow their bliss"—but not self-destructively or unproductively. I am not speaking of anarchists, excessive narcissists or cold, cunning manipulators. As I try to show in this book, the creative adaptive person functions effectively and helpfully to the degree to which he or she touches (or is touched by) "unitive consciousness." I explore this lucid, boundless, non-dual awareness in each chapter, defining it in Chapter 1.

I describe creative adaptation in some detail in my book *Living*

Happily Ever After. In this book, I examine the manner in which the creative adaptive mind demonstrates its own higher unitive consciousness. The elevated, heightened awareness of the psychosocial dimensions of the creative mind has been of interest to me for almost three decades. For example, in 1979 I first outlined the way in which creatively gifted or self-actualizing adults differ in thinking from their traditional-minded peers (Sinetar, 1980, pp. 749–55). I originally used America's workplace as my arena of focus in this matter. In the most general terms, in the seventies my observation was that anyone with eyes to see could observe a global shift in thinking and perception. What social scientists called a "paradigm shift," I saw as a collective rise in unitive consciousness. In Chapter 1, then more generally in subsequent chapters, I restate my perspective about the elements of this shift. To me, we are moving from an egocentric, fragmented perception— the childish perspective that "sees in part"—to a clear, synergistic, whole-seeing mind that "does away with partial things."

I propose that the world's increasing interest in spirituality is yet another signpost pointing to growing numbers of people influenced by unitive consciousness. Spirituality and spiritual insights are requisite, logical outgrowths of the creative adaptive mind. In this book, I discuss spirituality in secular terms so that even the unchurched or nonreligious might identify with, and find themselves in, these pages. This is a special challenge for me, since I myself am theologically inclined. The mind of which I write has many sides, is infinitely varied and deep, and I wanted to speak a language that would draw in and include the widest possible number of people.

When people fail in life, it is usually because they have not properly touched the hem of their own heightened awareness. They are disconnected from their own inner kingdom of riches. Chapter 2 suggests some ways in which Positive Structuring may address this deficit, and each subsequent chapter attempts to show how people might use the method to help develop their own creative adaptive minds.

Throughout this book, I interweave three related strands. First, I show how Positive Structuring lets us playfully simulate the creative process and brings us progressively useful insights necessary for resourceful problem solving. I describe why Positive Structuring helps us observe our own thinking. Next, I explain how Positive Structuring helps us develop creative adaptive skill by bringing us into lively, positive engagement with our own mental powers and with the problems that concern us. Gradually, imperceptibly, and imprecisely in most cases, we learn to trust our minds in the practical larger areas of daily life.

I do not suggest that Positive Structuring be used as self-therapy, or as a technique for those struggling to overcome dysfunction or serious emotional problems.* While clinical therapists, no doubt, will add this technique to their bag of favorite methodologies, Positive Structuring is not really a psychological method at all. Although it holds enormous potential to assist creative learning and problem solving, Positive Structuring evolved out of my own keen interest in art, architecture and construction. I have successfully applied these interests to finding business solutions for my clients for the past decade. Only recently have I come to appreciate the amazing application of this method to self-development. I have developed a constructive art that seems, over time, to raise consciousness.

As I show throughout this book, many people quietly experiment along these same lines on their own, without fanfare. Anyone who perseveres, those who try out this or that idiosyncratic approach to find tangible solutions or reach far-off dreams, may be less interesting to psychologists, researchers and the press than those whose lives express the high drama of psychological impairment or self-destruction. However, to me, the former are life's true, unsung, unrecognized heroes, because they continually manage to transmute negative forces into positive ones. These pages are full of illustrations of healthy, independent and resourceful thinkers whose minds seem full of light. We can study their examples, assessing ourselves in the process. But, I repeat, Positive Structuring is not a quick fix. It is a practice, perhaps an art. Certainly, it is a way of understanding the specific demands of our goals and a route to perceiving reality as one whole, exquisite fabric.

Although I describe Positive Structuring thoroughly in Chapter 2, I admit at the outset that the method is slippery, hard to quantify. I cannot say exactly *why* Positive Structuring works, provides answers, promotes personal growth—only that it does.

Both creative adaptivity and Positive Structuring move us toward unitive consciousness and spiritual growth, allowing what psychiatrist Reza Arasteh calls "final integration"—our ultimate development, our

---

*If a person is depressed or physically impaired, it is essential for him or her to get a clean bill of health from a physician before trying this or any self-improvement program. Since clinical depression is often biochemical or even genetic in origin and can masquerade as apathy, boredom, procrastination and low enthusiasm, a doctor's input is warranted if and when dysfunction is suspected.

full humanity. It is unitive consciousness—not my, or anyone's, technique—that seeds our final integration, spiritual insights and creative adaptation. There is mystery here because consciousness, our deepest mind, is involved. But this seems just one more riddle of existence to hold lightly and appreciate with wonder as we draw near the perfect.

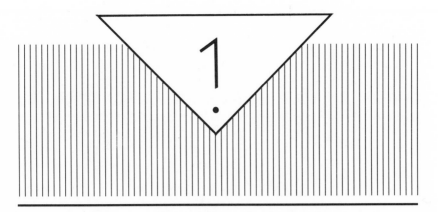

A 21st-CENTURY MIND IS CREATIVELY ADAPTIVE

The slave, in the spiritual order, is the [one]
whose choices have delivered him over,
bound hand and foot, to his own
compulsions, idiosyncrasies and illusions, so
that he never does what he really wants . . .
but only what he has to do.

THOMAS MERTON, *The New Man*

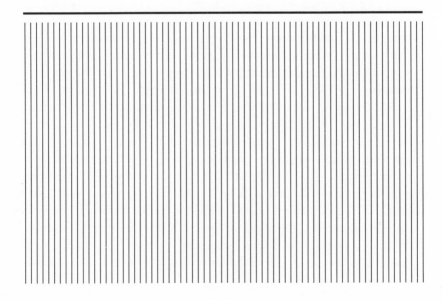

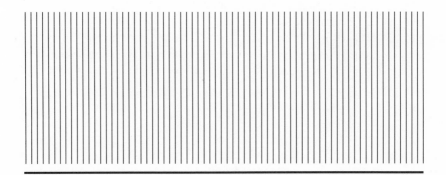

In my practice of organizational change management, senior executives in Fortune 500–type companies regularly tell me that they see their long-standing beliefs, stability and practices disintegrating. What once worked no longer does. Their authority is now undermined by either vocal, sophisticated employee groups or by abrupt change. Often they bitterly describe their own transfers or terminations from high-ranking functions because of restructurings or corporate mergers. One man faced such reshuffling twice in three years. "Yes," he admits, "I'm well compensated for this separation, but work—not money—is my primary means of fulfillment. At my age, it's not easy to be rehired. All I wanted was a secure position with long-term job security. Is that asking too much?" Yes, I reply. Today this is indeed asking too much.

If, like my client, we still yearn for orderly, predictable lives, we, too, may be losing touch with contemporary realities. A brief examination of America's disrupted workplaces reveals that mergers, acquisitions, restructurings and downsizings are making large organizations high-risk arenas for those who seek a "secure job with long-term job stability." Automation and robotization are, and will be, shrinking the work force further. If only in terms of our occupational life, most of us will be affected by some sort of upheaval as we enter the 21st century.

This is not to say that we are doomed to sell pencils on a street corner. Far, far from it. Ample and rewarding job opportunities exist in both small business and in newly emerging, internationally relevant entrepreneurial fields. By the year 2000, it is predicted that more than 70 percent of Americans will be engaged in some form of entrepreneurial work. By the end of the next century, almost all countries will have entered some form of *post* industrial culture. These two trends alone suggest luxuriant options for living arrangements, work choices and economic gain. But before we can be attractive job candidates in new fields or take advantage of opportunities springing up everywhere, we must rise far enough out of routinized mental ruts to be able to *see* fresh alternatives.

This fresh approach could be termed "personal reinvention" or personal entrepreneurship, and it has many faces and variables. For some, this state encourages a forward move into untried arenas of greater complexity. For others, simplifying life (a seemingly backward step) is the order of the day. Those who still seek formulas for quick-fix, instant solutions search with the wrong mind.

Not only corporate clients but others, too, report that they get stymied by what their entrepreneurial peers see as "opportunity." One individual, representing hundreds of others, wrote to say that although she was well trained and educated, the thought of making a transition into a new career left her with more questions than answers.

> I'm forty-five, have a Ph.D. and all my life have been a good student and employee. I'm a good follower of other people's rules. That's been my success formula. Now this formula doesn't work.
>
> As I read your books, I resonate with a part of myself that yearns to be more self-expressive, but I don't know how to let that part out. I'd like to work with corporations as you do, in my own field, of course. What course work could you recommend? How long do you think I'd have to study before I could go out on my own?
>
> As I read my own questions, I wonder if I'm not "overeducated," since I automatically assume that more school is my answer. What do you think?

Essentially, such comments fall into two distinctly different categories: those that represent the "Haves" and those that represent the "Have Nots." The Haves know their answers reside in them. They discover ways to draw these out. We can call such self-reinvention by any number of names: for example, personal entrepreneurship or creative adaptation. What counts is not the label but the particular response style.

Have Nots still believe that only traditional routes hold their answers (like formal schooling that results in degrees or certification). Or they search for quick-fix, prescribed solutions from without that tell them "how" to move through transitions. In stressing the power of tradition or the insight of others, they think along outdated lines.

Changing social mores, altered demographics, economic ills, the

aging of society, worldwide environmental concerns, changing political boundaries, international drug wars, new, lethal viruses—these
realities present new and special problem-solving challenges. Even current dislocations in family systems and cultural institutions intimately
envelop each of us in change. For this we need minds capable of bright,
21st-century thinking. With chilling clairvoyance, futurists prophesied
decades ago that adaptation was a personal survival necessity—not just
a narcissistic, self-help luxury. However, few have focused on the way
in which thinking skill—specifically illuminated whole-seeing—supports creative adaptation.

CREATIVE ADAPTATION AS PERSONAL REINVENTION

Creative adaptation generates personal reinvention and develops inner
balance, self-trust, experimentation and the blossoming of intuitive
intelligence. It implies continual, appropriate adjustment to a changing
field of opportunities—not a onetime response to a single disruption.
Creative adaptors continually accommodate practical realities while
also having the ability, adroitness and courage to ask the world to
accommodate itself to them. Another name for creative adaptors might
be "personal entrepreneurs." An entrepreneur manages, organizes,
strategically plans and executes the demands of a business or enterprise.
Similarly, creative adaptors manage, organize, strategically plan and
execute the pressures of day-to-day living in ways that meet, rather than
thwart, their own personal needs, values and goals. If, like my readers
or clients, they lose a job, they quickly land on their feet. After sifting
through the facts of their circumstances, they innovate their way toward their best answers.

Radical change and personal transitions are ideally made with an
improvisational, "no-blueprints" mind. For this, we need an artist's
faculty for blending our intuitive, nonlinear intelligences with our
strategic, rational ones. The best artists think along concurrently innocent and deliberate lines. Their minds are simultaneously open and
closed. They may be uncompromising, perhaps even have a child's
stubbornness when it comes to their preferred channel of aesthetic
value or vision, but they are receptive and eager for anything and
everything that assists self-expression. I propose that artists' spontane-

ous thinking flair, when they possess this, is a result of their perhaps natural awareness of pure consciousness.

No two artists understand or use the techniques of their work in exactly the same way. Similarly, there is infinite variation among all people in the way they perceive, interpret, analyze or act on data. Each of us possess what has been called "languages of thought." (John-Steiner, 1987, pp. 8, 11) We combine these languages idiosyncratically, but most of the time are unaware of our mind's functions. We don't realize when we mix or shift mental gears and, generally, have no feel for what these gears are. To strengthen creative adaptive skill, we must first become more deeply aware, so that we understand the pattern of our mind's thought-languages and learn to be fluent in all its dialects. As we increase our ability to "see" our mind's processes, we steadily gain control over both internal and external events.

What works for us intellectually speaking, in one time and circumstance may not work for anyone else or at another time. In today's world, certainly in tomorrow's, every situation calls for completely novel solutions. Unlike uniform, assembly-line thinking, precisely measured formulas and cookie-cutter outcomes, creative adaptive minds seek one-of-a-kind answers and believe, "If I can't solve this problem one way, I'll try another." Thus, by "control" I do not mean we should rigidly try to anticipate the future or prepare ourselves in advance with some kind of packaged, instant-solution kit. I mean we can be empowered if we know our minds are able, if we trust our insights.

The most effective expert minds figure out some things alone. And this is part of the fun. Novelist and critic John Gardner reminds us that, ultimately, no one teaches artists "how" to do their art: "The arts . . . can be taught up to a point; but except for certain matters of technique, one does not learn the arts, one simply catches on." (Gardner, 1985, p. 17) In the final analysis, all of us—not just artists—have to catch on. Creative adaptive minds catch on quickly.

True masters of this art tire and lose interest when ready-made, predigested solutions are handed to them. The artist Ben Shahn once said, "If I had a complete image I would lose interest in it."

Many creative adaptives admit that they relish exploration and the discovery process and say they hate doing the same thing twice. Creative adaptors enjoy, are easy with, the soft, shadowy underbelly of human existence, however illogical it may seem. Feelings, intuitive hunches, moods, dreams, personal preferences are their allies. They court the world of the "irrational." Strange as it seems, such persons become invigorated when tested in meetings with the unknown. However complex all this may sound, we all can apply the principles of this art to our own lives by practicing with small, unimportant dilemmas. This soon becomes an art of life—a way of opening up the doors to our mind's workings.

CREATIVE ADAPTATION AS THE ART OF LIFE

Creative adaptors study, some no doubt ultimately perfect, what we can only call the art of life. As master artists, they assume responsible roles. By this I mean they consciously choose to live with (and may wholeheartedly delight in) the consequences of their actions. Their minds share many characteristics; chief among these is a love of discovery. Such minds:

- are objectively aware—can transcend or move beyond themselves;
- are willing to think independently;
- have a high tolerance for change, discontinuity, paradox;
- are nonentrenched, inclined to release habitual beliefs and behaviors once these prove unproductive;
- trust experimentation—if they can't do something in one way, they try another.

Someone who wants to live in the country, who hasn't the background or means to earn a living there, yet manages to figure out how to survive and perhaps even thrive in a rural community, is a creative adaptor. So is the person who figures out how to join a corporate work team despite the lack of credentials or track record, or the one who changes careers late in life to follow a long-cherished dream. All will love the lengthy, winding process of figuring out "how" to achieve their goal. Moreover, they will relish life once their goal is reached. Like a sixty-year-old who told me he is thrilled to be starting a community service project providing health care for the poor, creative adaptors tend to love the climb up the mountain, as well as the arrival itself. "I'm enjoying this phase of personal exploration," said a woman who wasn't sure what her next job was to be. "It's as if I need a time-out period in which to play with many possibilities and interests." Experimentation is a key to finding answers.

In sum, the art of creative adaptation demands and depends on learning resourcefulness, is more than mere adjustment to the status quo and breeds its own inventiveness. This response is free-styled, highly individualized and solution-driven, and rejects trite, preconceived answers.

Because the term *creative adaptation* connotes, among other things, entrepreneurship, enterprise, tactical foresight, a mix of strategic planning and childlike intuition—what I call "shrewd innocence"—self-confident people (and perhaps predominantly those with high achievement drives) have the advantage. Enjoying the process as much as the results, personal entrepreneurs initiate action quickly and vigorously. Theirs is an active art that also demands periods of non-doing, reflection, passive or open receptivity to new ideas, the incubation of a big-picture vision, a tactical plan and the details to work the plan.

Overall, creative adaptors are self-governing, independent and decisive. They are happier when figuring things out alone, and enjoy the feel of their own brains at work. "I could sit in a room alone all day," a creative adaptive executive once said. "I get visceral pleasure as my brain works on problems." She added that, ideally, she would like her secretary to slide these problems under her door, so that her thought processes could be left undisturbed.

Gifted creatives in all fields easily relate to this sentiment. I once read that William Blake hated to be bothered by the busy details of existence; apparently, his wife's chief role was to protect him from interruption. A friend of mine who buys, runs and grows businesses agrees. She prefers to work alone, undistracted by others or by conversation. In just this way, those who want a creative adaptive mind must learn to *enjoy* their independence, and have fun with problems, even when they work in teams or on team projects. A creative adaptive mind interprets problems as stimulation and as challenge.

People who successfully change careers in mid-life with little or no direction from others also have creative adaptive minds. So does anyone who is ill and who bravely experiments with various mental or physical adjuncts to a traditional health care regime. Each is an adaptive artist in his or her own right, proceeding in much the same manner as writers, poets or sculptors who aren't sure exactly "how" to produce some desired result but who nevertheless explore different methods and "catch on" over time.

Job transitions, the creation of good health or nonconventional, unexpected life arrangements are more likely to succeed if we learn to respond creatively and with an experimental, fully engaged mind.

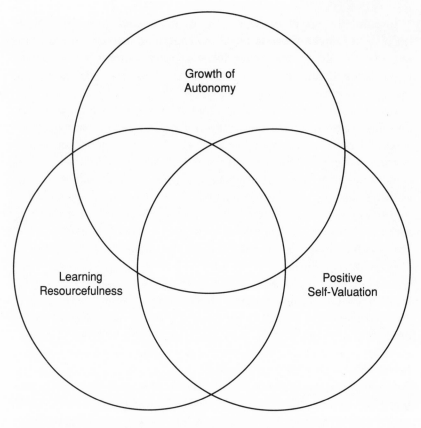

© 1990 Sinetar & Associates, Inc., Stewarts Point, CA 95480

ASSESSING OURSELVES AS CREATIVE ADAPTORS

Successful creative adaptors share many other traits: optimism, a willingness to take risks, self-confidence, inner balance and a love of freedom, especially in their professional field or area of interest. These traits in turn are linked to three clusters of skills that seem to underpin the creative adaptive response. (See Figure 1.) We can quickly assess, in general terms, whether or not we are developing creative adaptive skill. Questions like those that follow can evoke answers about our level of personal resourcefulness:

• Am I able to turn unexpected, unwanted events into something positive and productive?

- Do I have my own preferred way of solving problems, and would I call myself an *effective* solution-finder?
- Generally, do I think of problems or obstacles as challenges to my ability to take care of myself and achieve mastery over life?
- Have there been times in my life when, even though I didn't know exactly what to do, I knew in my heart I'd figure things out?
- Do I have the experience or the sense that even during a personal crisis I can function, know whom to ask for help, find my way?
- Have I ever let go of an old, outmoded way of thinking or doing something even though it was comfortable?
- Am I the type of person who enjoys experimenting? Can I move toward my personal professional goals without blueprints or guarantees of success?
- Can I ask for help from others when I need to without feeling inept or ashamed? Am I the kind of person who knows when to ask for assistance and when to figure things out alone?
- Do I sometimes just "play around" with possible answers, and can I sustain not knowing how things will turn out for a lengthy period of time?

When I first attempted to identify the skills that helped people manage change successfully or allowed them to respond effectively to life's ups and downs, I saw that exceptionally practical individuals did not so much adjust to the status quo as they somehow experimentally shaped things to their own vision of what was desirable. They apply a learnable cluster of behaviors that work synergistically in their favor. I call these skills because they are learnable. Chief among these are:

- positive self-valuation;
- resourceful learning;
- growth toward personal autonomy or independence.

Almost anyone has the capacity to develop these skills since none of these depends on age, education, cultural or socioeconomic background, gender or degrees of privilege—although the younger we start practicing, the better. Moreover, creative adaptation is a perceptual set that stimulates effective functioning. The person who sees the world as plastic and quite malleable is generally flexible himself. That individual's specific, nonrigid response style is grounded in skills and outward behaviors that influence attitudes, beliefs and self-view.

TRADITIONAL VERSUS 21ST-CENTURY THINKING

To better understand the differences between a traditional mind and what I call "21st-century thinking," it helps to recall the television antihero Archie Bunker. Bunker vividly and humorously caricatured the stereotypical, traditional mind alive in all of us. Bunker polarizes everything into good and evil. His truly is the perspective of the fruit of the Tree of Knowledge of Good and Evil. Archie defines "good" as all that of which he approves and "bad" as all that seems unlike or foreign to him. He is a veritable judgment machine, endlessly spewing out his pro/con evaluations about life. People, events, politics, his neighbors, religion, food, ways of life, dress or habits—all are subject to his same harsh scrutiny. Everything is fodder for his endless talk about virtue and sin, like and dislike, good and bad. This is dualism at its peak. It cuts the individual off from the present moment, thwarting life itself. Archie's emotions are heavily invested in things, people, events, ideas. His anger, hate, fear, resentment, preferences and opinions attach him to the world and split his spirit apart. Archie is an observer who views all else as an object. When we laugh at Archie, of course, we are laughing at ourselves.

By contrast, the Zen master Dogen illustrates a nondual mind. Thought to be one of the first to teach that life is an integrated whole, Dogen believed it is we, in our own self-limiting way, who fragment reality into pieces with our judgment and preferences. He taught that each instant should be perceived as a totality, that means and ends do not exist, that the here and now is an end in itself:

> . . . if there were a bird that first wanted to examine the size of the sky, or a fish that first wanted to examine the extent of the water and then tried to fly or swim, it would never find its way. (Bancroft, 1979, p. 22)

As we develop our own nondual thinking, we become less attached, less distracted, less polarized. Our emotional investment in circumstances and our judgmental tendencies lessen. This is not to say we don't care about things, but that we join more fully into the stream of life, instead of separating ourselves from it. We live in an alert, aware and present state. This invites specific, positive life-energies that support productive thought and action. We must not mistakenly think that nonduality implies that people, matter or ideas just bleed together without differentiation like a blur of watercolors painted on a too-wet page. Those with what I've called whole vision do not live in a blissed-out stupor or in a world of LSD-like hallucination. Quite the opposite. They possess deep clarity, experience the interconnectedness of all living systems and their holistic consciousness enhances their relationships to others and to the world. Maharishi Mahesh Yogi's statement that everything has its origins in one absolute existence puts this mind in yet another frame.

J. D. Salinger's fictional character, Teddy, epitomizes another stereotypically non-dual mind. Salinger clothes this topic in contemporary garb. Teddy is a fully enlightened being in a child's body. We see in this disheveled youngster the same exquisite perceptual field that the poets Rumi, William Blake or E. E. Cummings reveal in their works and the same healthy world-view that Emerson, or Martin Buber, or the saints, mystics and geniuses of science, art and leadership express in their particular ways. Teddy sees people and the world's variables against an ever-present background of an invisible, indivisible cosmic reality. This unseen backdrop is felt or experienced to be the true nature of things, and so excessive subjective investments in people or things are unnecessary, perhaps impossible. When he contemplates his own death, which he does even at six or seven, Teddy is not "always sticking emotion into things that have no emotion." This boy does not attach himself unproductively even to God: "Sure I love Him, but I don't love Him sentimentally. . . . If *I* were God, I certainly wouldn't want people to love me sentimentally, it's too unreliable." (Salinger, 1953, p. 187) Once we grasp the nature of Teddy's lucidity, we ourselves can find evidence of it everywhere and can see traces of it in almost everyone. Only the nondual mind promotes creative adaptivity, since personal autonomy, positive self-value and learning resourcefulness flourish under its influence. This mind promotes our richest spiritual faculties as well, inducing a kind of gratefulness of heart. On those days when everything is going right for us, when for no apparent reason we feel happy to be alive, we are probably close to, or in, this state of mind.

CREATIVE ADAPTATION AS A "LIFE TOOL"

In many people, the qualities, attitudes and abilities needed for successful creative adaptation remain latent. For its development, daily practice is needed. It is important to bear in mind that creative adaptation
is an art practiced loosely—not with precise, mechanistic techniques,
or in any one way. The pliant qualities of flexibility, imagination and
belief systems are tools that help us grow into creative adaptivity. All
these can evolve into *skills*. Belief, imagination and intuition, for example, seem to me "life tools." We can enhance these and employ them
to our advantage. The more we practice, the stronger our own life tools
become. In other words, even if we do not now possess much creative
adaptive skill, we can and should exercise—get into shape.

When the Irish novelist Christy Brown was just a child, he realized
that he was somehow different from other children. Born with cerebral
palsy, the boy was unable to speak, walk, feed or dress himself. He
could move only his left foot. With determination, endless practice and
the application of his imaginative, bright mind, Brown taught himself
to read, paint, type and express himself so expertly that he became a
major literary figure. Brown described the freedom his efforts brought:

> [When I was writing] I wrote and wrote without pause without
> consciousness of my surroundings hour after hour. I felt a different
> person. I wasn't unhappy any more. I didn't feel frustrated or shut
> up any more. I was free, I could think, I could live, I could create.
> . . . I felt released, at peace, I could be myself. . . . And if I couldn't
> know the joy of dancing I could know the ecstasy of creating.
> (Brown, 1989, p. 175)

Brown's success, his cultivation and expression of his lavish humanity, shows us what can be accomplished through effort and creative
adaptivity. Beneath the surface of all creative adaptives' self-development or achievements, we find three critical, life-supporting skills:
positive self-value, learning resourcefulness and the growth toward
autonomy. Fortunately, these capabilities can be learned.

POSITIVE SELF-VALUATION

Positive self-valuation is precisely and simply what it says: the ability to hold ourselves in high regard. It is our value of who we are and who we are becoming. We adopt this "idea of self" in early childhood, and hold the idea intact by our subsequent thoughts and actions. People with high self-esteem internalize the belief that they are likable, competent, worthwhile and powerful. By "powerful" I mean they feel themselves innately capable when faced with difficulty; they know, even if they have no obvious present solution, that in time they will figure out "how" to solve a problem. Self-trust is thus another key aspect of the creative adaptive response.

Positive self-valuation is *not* egotism or hubris, but rather is enlightened self-acceptance. As we accept our faults, shortcomings or failures, and acknowledge these in the true spirit of self-forgiveness, our generous attitude lets us move on to become the improved, self-mastering person that our high, healthy self-esteem demands.

LEARNING RESOURCEFULNESS

To fulfill this goal, we are willing to learn new things and to apply our understanding to other aspects of life.

To live effectively in a changing world means integrating previous learning into the process of our current-day life. Creative adaptives are self-educating and strive for application of what they already know in better, improved ways. Their learning is both a process that relies on multiple, distinctive skills *and* a life-stance characterized by openness to knowledge, self-questioning and flexibility. Sounding much like Christy Brown, a woman who extricated herself from a loveless, abusive marriage said, "I wake up in the morning thinking, 'Life is good,' and fall asleep feeling, 'I am truly blessed.' That is not to say I don't have problems, but I'm learning to handle what comes up and know now that I can trust myself. This learning is a small price to pay for happiness."

Resourceful learning involves a host of higher-order thinking skills, but does not so much depend on set IQ points or formal education as it does attitudes and ways of using information. Too much or too strict a formal education can actually interfere with resourceful learning.

Resourceful learning depends on possessing the knack of gathering and processing information as well as on having motivation or mental energy to follow through on often-difficult long-term tasks. A good friend, on relocating his home and new business to another city, said he had never worked harder. "I don't know what I'm doing, but I have the feeling that if I just play around, experiment with this transition, somehow things will fall into place. I take it a step at a time, regroup a lot, rest as much as I can and plod on. Answers pop up when I least expect them. It's like being in graduate school again."

Effective learners may seem inconsistent, for they often change their minds. Since they enjoy discovering, they also crave the state that stimulates it—namely, *not-knowing.* They quite happily embrace chaos, especially in those areas that relate to their interests or chosen vocations. Then they try to order that confusion in fresh, creative ways. As we review the qualities of creative adaptors, we see that part of the continuum of their inventive process includes being able to use what they already know (and what already exists) to meet unusual or unpredictable events.

Creative adaptors do not change for change's sake or look for ways to reinvent the wheel. If anything, they use proven and familiar habits, traditional systems and routines, to stabilize life, especially during major transitions. For instance, an elderly woman told me when it became clear that she had to earn a living, although already well into her seventies and in frail health, she created a modest editorial business in her home because this was what she knew how to do. Her learning resourcefulness let her use past skills and knowledge as a tool. The creative adaptive person applies data, skill and past and present experiences with a spontaneous flair, whatever the situation.

To develop a creative adaptive mind, it helps to come to grips with how we, as unique individuals, think, imagine and learn, since creativity and learning are but two sides of a single coin. Resourceful learners use their ability to transcend their own thoughts in order to see the big picture and, whenever necessary, discard outmoded ways of thinking in favor of more appropriate ones. Their thinking processes are open to the influence of their nonconscious, intuitive selves. They daydream, incubate ideas and trust themselves to listen inward. This tendency of mind and spirit frees them from the bonds of what-has-been and from the expectations of peers, parents, society and institutions, thereby providing fresh insight and uncannily right directions.

GROWTH TOWARD AUTONOMY

In each society, part of the enculturation process involves teaching children to perceive, and believe in, the worldview of that particular culture. For instance, as young children learn their culture's sacred values or beliefs by heart, these imprint themselves on their minds. Similarly, gender roles and customs are prescribed for children while they are still infants. These lessons, unless transcended later, provide a clear blueprint for behavior into adulthood. On the other hand, as we become autonomous, we are becoming "that self which we truly are," as Kierkegaard phrased it. This self is true unto itself, accepts no external rule book as its sole guide, is self-governing. As our autonomy increases, we feel free to question authority, seek out our own answers or values, experiment and initiate action on our own behalf. Even under the best of circumstances, such liberated behavior is rarely easy. Without this drive toward independence and the social transcendence it entails, we never learn to think for ourselves.*

This does not mean the autonomous person lives on an island or does everything alone. An essential part of the mind that permits creative adaptation involves productive relationships, knowing how and where to find help and advice, and sensing how one's unique capabilities complete and serve others. At the same time, this mind intuits how others might complete or compensate for one's own limitations. Autonomous people view other people as family, teammates or as community, but not as gods or superhuman rescuers. Healthy inter-independence gives them the relational strength needed to find or invent their own solutions. As we grow autonomous, our innate, constructive mental abilities grow, too.

Creative adaptors enjoy developing and using their own insights because they delight in their perceptions as well as in their independence. They trust their own responses. In them we clearly see how the three skills I have just described operate synergistically, as a cluster.

---

*For a fascinating overview of the relationship between rigidity, low self-esteem and dependency on the one hand, and flexibility, healthy self-esteem and autonomy on the other, see *Autonomy and Rigid Character* by David Shapiro.

A MASTER AT WORK

A building contractor and fine blues guitarist whom I'll call John nearly severed all four fingers of his left hand in a construction accident. I heard about John from a friend, and believe he is quite obviously a master artist of creative adaptation. John not only embodies the three attributes mentioned above but also shows us why these are essential to life as an "art." After several operations, John's hand was intact but badly scarred, inflexible and very weak. His doctors told him he would never regain full use of his hand, and that has proved to be true. John says he intuitively knew that fact from the start. Nevertheless, he was determined not to give up his music. He couldn't play as he originally had, but he expected to do it another way.

John approached his problem from several directions simultaneously. He religiously performed all the exercises his physical therapist recommended. He took large doses of vitamin E to help alleviate scarring. He researched alternative methods of strumming the guitar and practiced a minimum of one hour daily, no matter how discouraged or frustrated he got.

John's case illustrates how closely enmeshed and mutually supportive positive self-valuation, autonomy and learning resourcefulness are. Without positive self-valuation, he would not have enough faith in his ability to play again, or to make it through the down times. Inner balance, self-control and optimism are added—all helpful qualities in the constellation of skills surrounding the creative adaptive composite. With self-trust and healthy self-esteem, we gain sufficient perspective to know that we *can* make a difference in our own lives. When tired or discouraged, for example, those with positive self-valuation tell themselves they'll feel better in the morning. These traits are allies enabling John to discount nay-sayers and experts who tell him it is best for him simply to accept his fate. John's autonomy breeds freedom.

When John was coming to terms with his new reality, he took calculated risks based on integrating new knowledge into his everyday life. He is now playing music that is more his own creation, more in his own unique, fine style than the music he played before his accident. John's creative adaptive response illustrates how we can continually strengthen ourselves, how our progress and development become integral parts of our enhanced life.

While researching the creative adaptive response, I saw clearly that creative adaptors *use* every challenge as a spur to their growth as human beings. As John demonstrates, not only do they meet and conquer novelty, but—by using and developing this complex of skills—they increase their personal power and influence. They develop the underlying expectation that the world *will* meet their needs. Their optimistic expectancy enhances their mental agility and generates problem-solving acumen.

When people view themselves as competent and able, their sense of being deserving and their ability to receive what they want expands. A self-fulfilling prophesy works on their behalf. Their anticipation and faith in what's possible accelerates proportionately. It is as if infinitesimal but courageous acts, even just a sliver of a positive thought, become the potent seed they themselves plant. In time this seed bears fruit. With this fruit, their faith in themselves expands. At the end of an intense day's workshop, one woman said, "I suddenly realize how capable I am. I must have forgotten—or looked the other way. But a moment ago, I experienced my own capabilities *as me.*" This direct experience lets us move into untried areas. Such insights surface as we put our attention on our strengths and "build up" faith in this perceptual mode.

I call this seed-planting, this small-step construction of what is desired, "Positive Structuring." The next chapter describes how to teach ourselves to playfully manipulate externals and our own nonconscious mental processes. Positive Structuring lets us feel we can create the life we want. This is because in small-scale, careful ways we watch ourselves doing just that: we build the "mind" or outlook that we desire.*

---

*This whole business of metaphorical thinking seems an idea whose time has indeed come. In his article "Praxsyma," BenYamin M. Lichtenstein writes: "The term 'praxsyma' derives from 'praxis' or practical action. . . . [this is] a philosophical move away from 'thinking about' or explaining a system, to experiencing or 'interacting with' a project. *In praxsyma, knowledge is generated through one's participation or involvement in a context of being or action.* Knowledge is not a static entity, nor is it abstract from the world. . . . " These passages came to my attention as I was editing this book for publication, illustrating, at least to me, that certain ideas are received by the collective consciousness as minds are ready to accept them. Relative to "praxsyma" or Positive Structuring, at least two (if not many) minds are thinking along the same lines. (See: BenYamin M. Lichtenstein, "Praxsyma: Tools for Creating a Just Society," *Proceeds, International Society of Systems Sciences,* 34th Annual Meeting, Portland, Oregon, 1990.)

CREATIVE ADAPTIVITY'S SPIRITUAL SIDE

The word *spiritual* implies any number of diverse drives. It can mean a tendency toward the ineffable seat of our emerging core self. It can mean a mystical sense, or a subtle perception of, or a feeling of, sacredness that drives our learning or self-healing—psychologically or physically. As was obvious in John's case, spirituality may simply push us toward life by demanding self-repair, tenacity in the face of hardship, goodness in the midst of evil. Or we might feel prompted to answer a radical call to heal the environment, relationships, our working life, an abusive past and so on. *Any* infusion of greater inspiration, love, kindness, positivity, patience or charity (factors that both Eastern and Western traditions and myths, fairy tales, Scriptures and poetry hold as "fruits of the spirit") indicates the presence of spirituality. Underneath all spiritual impulses is life, prodded along by our rising awareness that we love and choose to honor life, that we love and choose to honor sacred values such as beauty, truth, courage, justice or health. Spiritual drives make us want to touch what is deepest, most hidden, in ourselves. The closer we come to this hidden core, the more certain we can be that our spirituality will emerge and direct us, and that we will come to see ourselves—and others—as fundamentally good or decent.

Most assuredly, a higher consciousness infuses our emergence as whole-seers. Many names have been used to describe this awareness: cosmic, transcendent or Christ-consciousness, God-realization or self-realization. For this book's quite-general purposes, I prefer to use the term *unitive consciousness* to describe that force within each of us that transmits a boundless, oceanic and nondual sense of perception.

This high quality of being or "is-ness" is ascribed to all those whom tradition labels spiritual, such as clerics, mystics, seekers, esoterics or ascetics. But I see a larger population as spiritual. Artists, highly gifted creative problem-solvers, scientists, leaders, entrepreneurs, ordinary men and women with inventive or good-hearted qualities and even some unique children may all, in varying degrees, possess strong spiritual drives and maturity. I observe these traits in others all the time, even in those who do not consider themselves spiritual, who are not specifically religious or who shy away from vocabulary of this sort. As just one example of this, celebrated actress Glenda Jackson shows us the links between our own values (or sentiments) and our spirituality. In an interview Jackson describes the way in which truly great theater portrays what she terms our "divine individuality," and reminds us that we must cherish human life. Her remarks help us see that whenever people address themselves to such person-centered values as compassion, love, kindness or the sanctity of life (i.e., human, animal, environmental, etc.) they speak the language of spirituality—the heart's own tongue:

> I am not religious; I am probably an atheist. But I do believe in this divinity of human difference. . . . we have been given the task of living together *as* individuals on this little ball whirling away in space. How we choose to do this is the only thing that is important. . . . If a play is a good play it asks these questions and it helps us celebrate our differences. And it helps us not to be afraid. (p. 18, Winter, 1978)

Whether or not we think of ourselves as spiritual, if we identify with the constellation of skills, values and traits I'm describing here, we are probably developing along one or more lines of unitive awareness.

As an educator with long tenure in the secular domain, I am disinclined to link spirituality with religiosity, dogma or narrow, doctrinaire thinking. This does not mean that formalized religions lack spirituality. Despite variations, spirituality permeates Taoist, Buddhist and Christian precepts, as well as those of most other faiths. But for too long we have burdened the notion of spirituality with weighty, cumbersome and highly specialized theological language. William Blake's "For everything that lives is holy, life delights in life" is a simple, straightforward spiritual sentiment. The fully enlightened spirituality of the 13th-century poet Rumi runs along similar lines of mystery and wonder, although Rumi uses different, slightly veiled words to express his awe:

> Soul receives from soul that knowledge, therefore
> not by book nor from tongue.
> If knowledge of mysteries come after emptiness
> of mind, that is illumination of heart. (Arasteh, 1965, p. 111)

Lao-tzu boldly, clearly expresses this same mystery and spirituality in everything he writes: "There was something vague before heaven arose. How calm! How void! It stands alone, unchanging; it acts everywhere, untiring. It may be considered the mother of everything under heaven. I do not know its name, but call it by the Tao." (Ibid., p. 68) These are three different expressions praising one universally felt truth.

I wish we could expand our idea of spirituality and include far more people in our consideration of those having a morally elevated, high consciousness. Have we not already witnessed that this consciousness may be occuring in waves, among all peoples over all the world? This seems a sort of shared psychic revolution.*

This phenomenon has been called a "paradigm shift," and there is currently debate as to its causes. Some say technological improvements and geopolitical changes have expanded awareness, raised expectations and improved the quality of life to the extent that the globe will never be the same. Others describe the collective nature of the shift and feel it has moved beyond personal transformation. This move of spirituality clearly is not an either/or affair. As individuals, we are deeply transformed as we become self-actualizing. Communities, values and collective sensitivities are also altered to the degree that individuals gain emotional and psychological health.

Each month I receive numerous unsolicited letters from people, both churched and unchurched, describing their rich, enduring spiritual life. These individuals are like everyone's neighbors, families and friends. They include businesspersons, homemakers, students and every age, variety and type of individual. One woman's note, which I paraphrase, epitomizes hundreds of other personal testimonies:

> I began having spiritual experiences as a teenager. These, and the values that correspond to such interests, have strengthened throughout my life. I can best describe the experiences as a "union," as a floating or living in the soul of God. It is both awesome and humbling, one I wish everyone could experience.

Another correspondent wrote that he was motivated to work as hard as possible for community health. A third says, "I seem to be heading

---

*Marilyn Ferguson, Matthew Fox, Mark Satin, David Spangler, Alvin Toffler, are all examples of writers who have—over the last decade—described the changed consciousness of people around the globe.

toward service and away from strictly business—now I hope to be a service-oriented businesswoman." A fourth writes, "I'm feeling that my spiritual path is taking me into meaningful volunteer work in the environmental field. If there is a way to make money doing this, I'll be all the happier for it." In *Ordinary People as Monks and Mystics,* I provide a framework for the central values and motives that drive such choices. The point is that, historically, the issue of human spirituality has been shrouded in specialness and has inherited an insular quality. Yet people with well-developed spiritual faculties, whose minds see "whole," are often quite uncomplicated. A friend recently told me this story. It seems that a religious question was found scrawled on a wall of a major university:

And Jesus said unto them: "Who do you say I am?"

And they replied, "You are the eschatological manifestation of the ground of our being; the kermygma in which we find the ultimate meaning of our interpersonal relationship."

And Jesus said, "What?"

The spiritually mature possess, in some degree or another, a simple awareness of connectedness. This sense is not an intellectual matter but, rather, brings to their world feelings of relatedness. For the most part, the life of such persons is, to them, sacred, full of mystery and light.

Our rootedness in what is potentially universal and beyond ourselves as particular individuals stimulates the development of an interior life that sooner or later we may call "spiritual." For instance, while we usually think of Ho Chi Minh as a political, rather than a saintly, figure, his *Prison Diary* reveals another side of this leader. If we have open minds, we find much the same poignant, elemental or "heart-values" as in poets we do think of as spiritual. At the very least we can empathize with the feelings he expresses, and this creaturely feeling interweaves his and our life. This is spiritual.

The head warder at Pinyang has a golden heart.

He buys rice for the prisoners with his own money.

At night he takes off the fetters to let us sleep.

He never resorts to force, but only to kindness. (p. 77, Ho, 1971)

Spirituality also demonstrates itself as added zest. One person told me that her daily life gained added purpose as she grew in spiritual awareness: "My journey now has profound meaning, but not the kind the world acknowledges. Society's definition of success, a good career and relationship, is far different from what I want. Mine is the path toward the quiet. I seek God within me and within every life." Both spiritual growth and creative adaptivity require conversions of thought: these clarify, demystify, reveal to us our false views and limiting beliefs. Simply by taking "the path toward the quiet," such people automatically must think in novel, idiosyncratic terms. Their lives become creatively adaptive because often scaling-down or altering a traditional way means carving out a brand-new identity and set of values. Such carvings depend upon the skill of thinking for one's self.

For instance, independent thinking, the strength to speak one's mind or stand alone if one must, nonentrenchment, letting go of past habits and comforts or guarantees when necessary, are all signs of either spirituality and/or creative adaptivity. Both minds—the spiritual and the creatively adaptive—are receptive to emotional and material sacrifices; both minds recast standard relationships or revise work and lifestyles as growth demands.

The synergistic cluster of creative adaptive skills works together in ways that open us to what Maslow termed the "Being values." These are universally cherished ideas that, throughout history, mankind has esteemed. Beauty, truth, courage, joy, humor, creativity, spontaneity, love or compassion are all examples of the values we embody as we grow emotionally healthy. The greater our creative adaptation, the greater will be our immersion in such values. Furthermore, as we strengthen creative adaptive skills, we achieve a certain psychic homeostasis, or "inner peace." This, too, demonstrably converts perception, thought processes and behaviors. For example, in Chapter 3 we will see that intuition grows and is "heard," followed and trusted when people gain positive self-valuation and autonomy.

Our entire way of being is revised for the good as we adopt, develop and train our 21st-century mind. Love motivates and governs this mind. Joy increases. Despair diminishes. This mind becomes inventive, "transparent"—open to its own light, its realities and to the fundamental goodness of the core self—and feels friendlier toward the unknown. The individual faces his own darkness or unconscious processes, turns toward dreams and nightmares, tolerates unanswered questions, feels faithful to her own destiny, feels linked to others. Each adopts gentler, more peaceful means while slowly discarding harsh, aggressive drives.

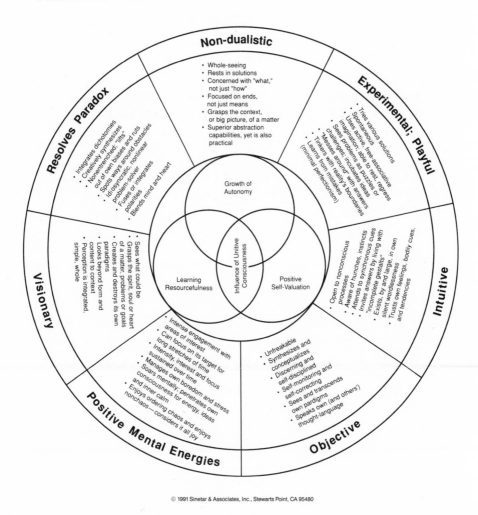

Non-dualistic
- Whole-seeing
- Rests in solutions
- Concerned with "what," not just "how"
- Focused on ends, not just means
- Grasps the context, or big picture, of a matter
- Superior abstraction capabilities, yet is also practical

Resolves Paradox
- Integrates dichotomies
- Creatively synthesizes
- Nonentrenched; "lifts" out of own biases and ruts
- Spots ways around obstacles
- Idiosyncratic, nonlinear problem-solver
- Fuses or integrates polarities
- Blends mind and heart

Experimental; Playful
- Tries various solutions
- Spontaneous, free associative
- Uses active imagination; able to rest, regress
- Sees problems as puzzles or challenges; incubates ideas
- Tinkers around with reality's boundaries
- Learns from mistakes (minimal perfectionism)

Visionary
- Sees what could be
- Grasps the spirit, soul or heart of a matter, problems or goals
- Creates and destroys its own paradigms
- Looks beyond form and content to context
- Perception is integrated, simple, whole

Growth of Autonomy

Learning Resourcefulness

Influence of Unitive Consciousness

Positive Self-Valuation

Intuitive
- Open to nonconscious processes
- Aware of hunches, instincts
- Attends to synchronous cues
- Invites answers by living with "incomplete gestalts"
- Exists, by and large, in own silent wordlessness
- Trusts own feelings, bodily cues, and tendencies

Positive Mental Energies
- Intense engagement with areas of interest
- Can focus on its target for long stretches of time
- Intensity, interest and focus sustained over time
- Manages over time boredom and stress
- Soars mentally; penetrates own consciousness for energy, ideas
- Enjoys ordering chaos and enjoys and inner calm nonchaos—considers it all joy

Objective
- Unfreakable
- Synthesizes and conceptualizes
- Discerning and self-disciplined
- Self-monitoring and self-correcting
- Sees and transcends own paradigms
- Speaks own (and others') thought-language

In the late seventies, I first outlined this shift, using America's workplace as my focus. (Sinetar, 1980, pp. 749–55) As noted, traditional minds and 21st-century minds differ in the most basic and obvious ways.

Of course, minds only change as individuals do. Spiritually maturing, creatively adaptive people, influenced as they are by unitive consciousness, begin to be reborn and transformed. Their perceptual field is altered, we might even say *illumined*. The psychiatrist Dr. Reza Arasteh describes this state as "final integration." These autonomous, fully human people are so private, hidden, ignored by, or perhaps even

Traditional Mind	*21st Century-Unitive Mind*
• Egocentric frame of reference	• Synergistic frame of reference
• Split-perception: sees the part; confused by paradox; centers on the detail	• Whole-seeing: first sees whole (contextually), then understands part; resolves paradox, dichotomies
• Polarizes and separates; feels disconnected, cut off from; alienated	• Integrates, unifies (feels itself part of the whole)
• Fear-motivated	• Love-motivated (agapé)
• Dualistic	• Non-dual

unknown in, our society that they sometimes seem nonexistent. When we find them, and be assured we can, we see that they have the power to stand on their own feet and determine their own life according to their higher light and spirit. Chapter 2 discusses one circuitous method for developing such autonomy and luminous power.

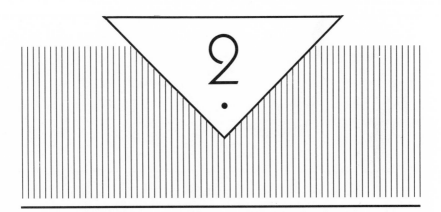

A 21st-CENTURY MIND PLAYFULLY SOLVES PROBLEMS

There is a Hindu myth about the Self or
God of the universe who sees life as [play].
But since the Self is what there is and all
there is and thus has no one separate to play
with, he plays the cosmic game of
hide-and-seek with himself . . . all the time
forgetting who he really is. Eventually
however the Self awakens from his many
dreams and fantasies and remembers his true
identity, the one eternal Self of the cosmos
who is never born and never dies.

R. H. BLYTH, Games Zen Masters Play

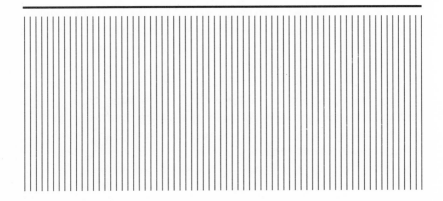

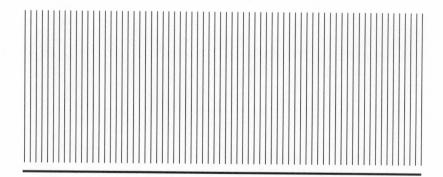

For some years now, I have happily experimented with a method for teaching my corporate clients about creative adaptation. It also seems to help them translate personal goals into concrete achievements, but is more about how to "be" and think than it is about how to "get." I now call the method *Positive Structuring*. It is my formalized attempt to show people how to think about their thinking. If creative adaptation is an art, then Positive Structuring is a technique or a practice to help us master this novel art form. Positive Structuring draws us into independent, creative thinking while simultaneously addressing our specific goals or transition concerns.

POSITIVE STRUCTURING: AN INTRODUCTION

I define Positive Structuring as a multifaceted, creatively constructive and highly individualized approach to personal change and accomplishment. Its method involves the creation of practical metaphorical models of those things we hope to have: solutions, qualities, conditions or material things. We first create and fuel of our desire in our imagination. Then, as our understanding grows, we build models or prototypes of these in real-world, low-risk, concrete and representational terms. When working with individuals in executive development sessions or with entrepreneurs who seek unusual answers to service or product-development questions, I find it beneficial to direct them to their own answers rather than to supply them with my own. In the early days of my practice, I generated useful answers for others. But I did not like to hear myself pontificating, being an advice-giver, creating dependencies instead of self-sufficiencies. In truth, I found advice-giving dull. When these sessions were completed, people still didn't possess the essential means or mental processes to solve their future problems. They continued to believe that I had some knowledge they lacked. This was not true. They had all the necessary tools, talent, insight and creative power, but simply hadn't developed a method for deploying these. My challenge was to devise a method that could teach individuals how to teach themselves to be creative while also enhancing their autonomy and self-esteem. I believe Positive Structuring is just such a tool.

Positive Structuring invites us to play our way into our best future, into those states, goals or circumstances that we desire. Whatever it is we hope to be, do or have, we must first give birth to the rudiments of our solution—must *positively structure* it—in our consciousness. We come to grips with the nature of the thing we want, release our hold or fixation on our problem or on that which threatens us. Inventively, we begin to live in our solution, to see our daily world from the vantage point of its essence. Then, in progressively more tangible steps, as much as we are able, we translate our initial imagery (our mind, feeling-pictures, or interiorized symbols) into concrete, physical forms. Much as architects create models of the buildings they plan to build, Positive Structuring involves us in building material or experiential solutions, helps us "have" rather than not-have, lets us gradually extinguish our troubles as we increasingly rest in the best solutions imaginable. This focus on solutions amounts to our registering a new pattern of possibility in our awareness. We reside in solutions first by using our imaginations to enter the world of our answers and later by realistically extending these mental "pictures" into the world at large.

Here we find the subtle, as well as the obvious, nature of our objectives. As we imagine solutions and create small-scale, tangible models that represent these, our awareness about answers expands. Light from our own mind expels the darkness of our concerns and ignites new ideas, optimism and faith in what we can accomplish. Over time, we alter our thinking about problems and begin to know ourselves in an improved way. If, for instance, we want to become creatively adaptive, we begin by simply mulling over what this phrase means *to us* in everyday terms. Then, selectively and on a progressively complex scale, we practice some of these attitudes and behaviors in a recreational, playful and private way. We need not discount the process, or ourselves, by making fun of it in social conversation or sabotage its potential by using high-risk settings (say, our workplace) for practice. Generally, Positive Structuring depends on several conditions, chief among which are these:

- *Active imagination.* Our mind must accept and "own" the idea of our goal; we use our imagination to identify it and help detail its characteristics.
- *Low-risk facsimiles.* We break up goals or problems into manageable bits. If we want greater autonomy, we might shop, attend a lecture or party alone, or take a short trip by ourselves. We do not move to another town or country or walk down a dark alley at night in order to create study models of independence and autonomy.
- *Small steps.* Our models activate elements, not the entirety, of what we want. If, say, we know we need self-discipline, we do not attempt to gain this wholly overnight. This is like swallowing a whole steak in one bite, whereas Positive Structuring asks us to thoroughly chew up and digest tiny bits of an idea or ambition before taking on more.
- *Gradational tasks.* Impatience is the mark of immaturity and having an idealized notion about what real adult growth entails. Often our impatience reveals low self-esteem and a tendency toward self-destruction. Instead, we must design a hierarchical program to methodically teach ourselves discipline.* We factor out the elements of whatever trait we want, then practice these much as if we were learning a sport, dance or art.
- *Registration.* Registration (Horney, 1950) means we notice and document what we can do and what we are doing, rather than focusing or registering what we lack or cannot do. Each time we complete a project, we automatically register this fact. Positive Structuring enhances adult growth because it inhibits the tendency to rush along unconsciously, while cultivating the positive habit of noticing small, productive acts and achievements. If somehow we reward ourselves after each step or model, so much the better.
- *Construction.* Positive Structuring involves a buildup, or seeding, of specific solution bits. First in our awareness, then later in physical or experiential terms, we assemble components of what we want while noticing, then processing out, our fears, misunderstandings and resistances. The adage "What you focus on you get" helps describe this positive seeding work.
- *Rest, regression and "failure."* Intrinsic, useful, and a valued part of the overall learning process.
- *Integrative learning.* As we sequence our own inventive tasks, we

---

*Sybervision, for example, offers many commercial programs along these lines and specifically has a learning series on self-discipline (SyberVision Systems, Newark, California).

notice that we favor certain types of activities; over time we intro-
duce ourselves to our favored learning styles and integrate these into
one innate and unitive intelligence.

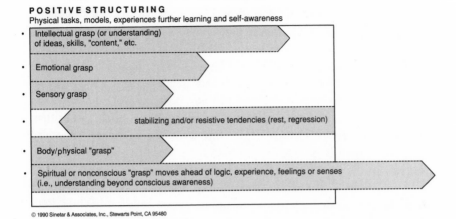

POSITIVE STRUCTURING
Physical tasks, models, experiences further learning and self-awareness

- Intellectual grasp (or understanding) of ideas, skills, "content," etc.
- Emotional grasp
- Sensory grasp
- stabilizing and/or resistive tendencies (rest, regression)
- Body/physical "grasp"
- Spiritual or nonconscious "grasp" moves ahead of logic, experience, feelings or senses (i.e., understanding beyond conscious awareness)

© 1990 Sinetar & Associates, Inc., Stewarts Point, CA 95480

SMALL STEPS SOLVE LARGER PROBLEMS

A client of mine I will call Pat knew she was rigid and unbending and
that she could not "go with the flow." She rushed meetings along at
work in order to end at precisely the right time. She restrained herself
when she had an impulse to talk, yet forced herself to speak up when
she had nothing to say. She felt judgmental, unbending and perfection-
istic. When she heard me describe Positive Structuring, she asked me
to help her design a study model. Her goal was to become more flexible
and innovative (both qualities exist within the synergy of the creative
adaptive skills complex). I explained that she was far better off designing her own models, but to get her started told her as much as I could
about the method.

At first Pat was baffled and found the technique obscure. But after
applying her imagination to the world of flexibility (i.e., her goal) she
came upon a model that she felt could help her develop the fluidity she
wanted. Pat decided she could enhance her flexibility by learning to
write with her left hand. Apparently, she had been taught to suppress
this ability in childhood. Pat's practice sessions helped her intimately
understand how she denied her body's impulses and held her own
intuition and resilience at bay. Practicing writing with her left hand
was by no means a panacea, merely an initial meditating device by

which she ruminated on how change might enlarge her capabilities and deepen her self-awareness. Pat's first model—altering a physical habit and preference—paved the way for larger changes and showed her what it meant to create physical extensions of her mind's goals.

Several weeks later Pat found another way to practice flexibility. This time she chose interpretive dance as an advanced vehicle to teach herself how to be effective in unstructured arenas. At first Pat was ashamed at her own awkwardness. She wanted her instructor to tell her exactly how to move to the music.* Her dance teacher and the other students encouraged her to relax, to find and trust her own way. Pat began to listen to and move to what she heard in the music rather than attend to others for cues of right and wrong. Her model—modern dance—helped her unlearn many habitual codes of conduct that she'd adopted in childhood.

In undoing her fixed patterns of response, Pat also increased her social adroitness; anxiety that arose in foreign settings diminished. Pat's study models were successful because she was fully involved and cared about her outcomes. In a similar way, as we fully grapple with low-risk projects that contain the seeds of some of the skills we want to learn, we, too, can grow.

I once heard a Tibetan monk say that a mantra keeps the mind safe, grips it enchantingly so that it isn't diverted into fearsome or ugly thoughts. In just this way, Positive Structuring models can grip our minds, hold our attention, transform our thinking and ultimately elevate awareness. Because we look for metaphorical models that are initially obscure, out of immediate reach, we engage our minds in an active, searching manner. This search, when coupled with high interest and personal motivation, approximates the creative process. Our mind comes into closer relationship with the spirit of our goal, much like that of growing intimacy with a lover or good friend. This search and this particular unfolding begin to show us that something in us knows, has answers. And as we become acquainted with our own awareness, we find playful, experimental ways to structure our wants—at least on a small scale and in representational fashion. These models let us honor

---

*Professor David Shapiro links rigidity to dependence on authoritarian rules or persons: ". . . flexibility—not rigidity—reflects a genuinely objective attitude toward the world. . . . The aims and purposes that rigid individuals impose on themselves, and live under ('I should accomplish more.' 'I should move.'), have precisely the character of established . . . imperatives." (pp. 75–76). Shapiro's point is that, when we are too rigid, rules ultimately replace our healthy, functional relationship with the external world.

our own pace, go as slowly as we must and work with our natural resistances.*

Architects, engineers, set designers, packaging scientists and product developers take courses to become trained in this method of using a scaled-down model to build the initial realities of what they hope to construct. To many, this must be science; to me, it seems art.

Positive Structuring also draws us into the depths of our own consciousness, lets us meet what is boundless and fluid in us. Eventually, we are influenced by the qualities of our awareness and get to know ourselves as possessing a creative spark, unique insight and problem-solving skill, energy, motivation and a strong life-force. Like Pat, as we meet the minute, ongoing change-field within, we learn that change can help us expand as individuals. Rather than fearing flux, we begin to dance with it—sometimes leading, sometimes following. Such mental fluidity greatly assists us in spotting the kinds of opportunities described earlier, whereas rigid thinking binds us unproductively to our own past and to our current knowledge.

THE THREE STAGES OF "PLAY": WHAT, NOT HOW

In general, Positive Structuring's "play" opens our thinking in three distinctive stages:

- First, we decide what we want, determine our target, identify where we want to go. We describe our goal or the solution we need in simple, general terms and begin to imagine the unimaginable.
- Next, we research this unknown. We try to enter into and understand the spirit and attributes of our objective whether it be attitude,

---

*Workshops, books and experts that force us to fight our fears with too-brutal techniques or confrontations seem barbaric to me. Parents who lack empathy for their child's fear of water, and throw them into the murky deep knowing full well their youngster is terrified, should learn to control themselves and their own anxieties. We, too, must control our tendency to "effort," to coerce ourselves into instant growth. Fear, as Moshe Feldenkrais wrote, is the one primitive emotion that stops us—"freezes us in our tracks like frightened animals." Unnecessarily courted, fear also prevents learning. Although superficially we move ahead, inside there remains fixation.

skill or something else: being more patient, saving money, learning to ski, finding new work, inventing a novel life or relationship solution.
- Then and only then are we ready to plan and design one or more "study models." These models are metaphors of, and represent, our target.

The first two stages involve understanding "what"—not "how." The model-building stage quite naturally progresses out of our expanded awareness about our goal that the first two stages generate. Each early phase of "play" readies and prepares us for the next. Many people rush through the first phases, but success in advanced stages (e.g., design of study models; building them) depends on effectiveness as learners in preceding stages. As we create low-risk, constructive models, our design process becomes a playful vehicle; the models and the process teach us about ourselves, are inseparable from our goal(s) and tell us "how" to extend ourselves further into our desired reality or objective. Robert Ludlum comments, ". . . if you think about doing something you should actually translate it as much as possible into physical terms." (Ludlum, 1982, p. 136)

I hasten to add that in its early stages Positive Structuring is not unlike psychological modeling methods (learning by imitation) by which we acquire or develop new, complex social skills by studying successful role models. At first, Positive Structuring does encourage us to locate admired role models. As we penetrate the spirit and essential elements of our objective, it helps to observe others who are doing or who have what we desire. However, this is where all similarity to modeling theory ends. Positive Structuring is not a "psychological" method, is not concerned with imitating behaviors or duplicating idealized states of mind or feeling. It is a thinking and building tool that lets our awareness reveal and make evident our own creative processes; these then lead us to our goals quite naturally.

Our inventions and study models show us concretely which thinking modalities or skills we favor. We intuit how our own way of learning optimally serves us—what works, what doesn't, what we enjoy, loathe, find easy or impossible, where we typically find ourselves asking for help, where, intellectually speaking, we lift off, move beyond what we know, even lead others. We also safely confront what we think we cannot be, do or have. Our beliefs become "readable" as we attend to our nuances of mind or objectively observe ourselves as thinkers. All the while we are seeding diverse aspects of our goal by focusing on what we want rather than on what we don't want.

The New Testament provides a parable about keeping our eyes on a prototype—an admired, effective model—and taking our eyes off our problems. Somehow control of attention aids coherence and develops faith in a mind otherwise distraught by trials. In the Book of Matthew (14:24–31), we read how the disciples, Peter in particular, yearn to walk on unruly, wind-tossed seas as Jesus does. Peter is commanded to simply get out of the little boat and start. He begins securely enough, but immediately, thinking about the dangers and glancing down at the black waters, ". . . he became afraid, and beginning to sink, he cried out . . . 'Lord, save me!' " To which Jesus replied, "O you of little faith, why did you doubt?" Christ's message is that when we want to tackle something we fear is beyond us, we must manage our mind and keep our eye on our target—not dwell on the dilemma.

With Positive Structuring, we are concerned with ends more than means. We continually think about the qualities of what we want rather than worrying too much about how to achieve it. Our whole mind settles into our objective. We then allow our small-scale models to show us our next steps; as we evaluate our effectiveness, we gain insight, realize how to advance, understand our motives. These experiments stimulate the "how"—let us play with methods and techniques of attainment—since we must actually meet the demands embedded in the models' construction. For instance, Pat learned about flexibility from concrete but totally private and nonthreatening projects. While addressing the realities of writing with her left hand and learning modern dance, Pat grew psychologically resilient—but no one in her workplace knew of her experiments.

Almost any trait can be learned in this unhurried, attentive and conscious way. If we feel overcommitted, mentally crowded or confused by an impending assignment or transition, we can first entertain a goal of orderliness. In imagination we try to flush out the behavioral qualities and real-life outcomes of a methodical nature. Next, we might create metaphors of this goal in tangible, low-risk models: We clear out our closet or garage, pay some accumulated bills or file an unruly stack of papers that we've avoided. In this elementary fashion, we soon slip through the limits and resistance that we place in our own way. Our models help our mind transcend its self-imposed obstacles, our fear of change or our erroneous belief in ourselves as "confused."

As we observe ourselves organizing our immediate environment, we realize we have the very traits we want: calmness, rationality, orderliness—even if only in emerging form.

People who have difficulty concentrating can adopt the same approach, act "as if" they had long, solid attention spans by finding projects that draw forth such traits. Their models could involve chess, word puzzles or other games that structure discipline and focus into consciousness. This process embodies the metaphysician's rule that our answers reside within the heart of our problem.

EXPERIENCING NEXT STEPS AND THE WORKINGS OF OUR OWN MIND

Just as an infant teaches itself about directions, weight or gravity by constantly dropping a spoon, so Positive Structuring's simulations open our awareness to our next-step learnings. We can use craft, architecture and construction projects to upgrade our understandings. We can use experiences that we ourselves design, as Pat did, to gradually improve our response styles or way of life, self-esteem and set way of being.

Positive Structuring helps us experience our own minds at work. Its tasks ask us to replicate the creative process. We use study models on the physical plane to expand and deepen our concentrative abilities and our imaginative powers. Our object is to create positive metaphors of aspects of the thing we want and thereby *study* the thing as we go. It is not the model or replica that matters so much but the reference that counts and the revelatory value inherent in it.

Numerous and diverse means help us: pictures, words, plastic, wood, our own daily life, actual "detective work" (e.g., reading about the goal, searching for role models or case illustrations) and later, as we advance, we build experiential or physical "systems" that metaphorically and actually teach us about the rules, truths or special requirements of the things we want. We so thoroughly acquaint ourselves with the endpoint, solution or transition that our total attention on it establishes a relationship with these. We move from outer (i.e., the goal) to inner (our imagination about it), back to outer (our projects and study models) and then back again. Each movement or turn of attention lets us weave back and forth between interior and exterior realities, bringing our inmost hunches or resonances to life so that our functioning improves in the area of concern. The process mysteriously develops both our human and our spiritual potentials.

If, for example, our goal is to save money, we can begin by putting ourselves in thought into a state of affluence. Our visualizations ultimately teach us about the specific laws natural to saving, thrift or increase. Soon and quite naturally, we'll begin to examine our daily habits in this area of concern. There may be ways in which we squander our resources—not just money, but time, talent and energy. Or we may see that our priorities are mixed and unruly. Who hasn't realized during some social event that this particular group or activity was a giant misuse of time? Who hasn't known that this or that energy-draining, mind-numbing relative, friend or business colleague had nothing to offer? Once we see how we waste ourselves, there are many practical things we can do to pull in the reins. Saving, spending and investing projects will each then have many sides and facets—all of which relate to our own idiosyncratic needs and patterns.

"CONSTRUCTING" A METAPHOR: THE FIRST STAGES OF SOLUTION ARCHITECTURE

Positive Structuring adopts a practice long used by designers, engineers and architects: the construction of three-dimensional models that act as guides. The point, at first, is to use study models to thoroughly comprehend ourselves and our goals that we minimize errors, risk-taking and emotional upheaval. We also determine what we are willing, or able, to pay for the probable costs of our efforts and ambitions.

Some people already understand how this works and do it naturally. For example, a client to whom I introduced Positive Structuring told me that she understood the method because earlier that year she'd used a computer model to teach herself about city planning. Instead of simply outlining theory, the software simulates urban development problems. My client solved these by applying city planning techniques. An unusually bright, able reader told me that he was teaching himself how to grow his business by using a software program in which simulations taught him how to forecast. He was forced to answer specific questions of time, risk and complex project requirements. Pilots, law enforcement officers and the military have all traditionally been screened, hired, developed and even retrained by using realistic imitations of airline, crime or war crises.

Although we are usually unaware of it, all of us substitute one entity or idea for another to help us describe or understand things. In their book *Metaphors We Live By,* authors George Lakoff and Mark Johnson outline how the conceptual systems of societies are grounded in physical experience. These quite naturally become metaphorical, and show us "how" to comprehend complicated cultural or theological concepts.

As we think about our own ambitions or transition projects, as we ask ourselves what self-instructive study models we might create, it is important to keep in mind that each Positive Structuring model must naturally link us to the outcome we want. The model is a relevant symbol. As a dove reminds us of peace, gentleness, or—to Christians— the Holy Spirit, so must our study models remind us, personally, of what we want to be, do or have. (Lakoff and Johnson, 1980)

One of the most exciting elements of Positive Structuring is its inherent difficulty. Because it is not easy to design a study model, because we are initially perplexed by having to come up with a metaphoric emblem of our solution, we are automatically pulled into a birthing process of invention.

"CONSTRUCTING" REALITY: THE LATER STAGES OF "PLAY"

Positive Structuring demands that we so fully identify with the creative principle itself, asks that we enter the reality of our aim with such complete absorption, fascination and commitment that the process replicates the mind and attention level of invention. At first, in consciousness, then gradually we experience concretely the mystic's awareness that we are the very solution we want—if only in our feelings, sympathies, or understandings. We do not wait around for mystical experiences or other worldly signals. Visions, ethereal lights or occultish signs are irrelevant and may be counterproductive. Nor do we try in any way to capture some special state or create artificial moods. Rather, we simply think about, toy with and experiment with physical and experiential models—symbolic equivalents of our goal—to school ourselves in their realities and "Positive Structure" them in our awareness. This draws us into beneficial thought patterns.

Through exploration, play and creative incubation and with physical or interactive projects as our self-styled teachers and study guides, we incorporate then transcend "mental equivalents." The mental equivalent, as metaphysician Emmet Fox so aptly taught, always comes first. But since we live in a material world—in a physical universe—we must also help ourselves evolve as people who function effectively in a complex and practical manner. In other words, it's not enough just to visualize or imagine something. Eventually, we have to take action, put one foot in front of the other, step out toward our goals. In the words of an entrepreneur friend, "At some point you have to get on with it."

THE PROCESS OF POSITIVE STRUCTURING: A SAMPLE CASE STUDY

Phase I: Getting Started

A client of mine whom I'll call J* needed to improve her ability to stick with tasks despite boredom. She was the sort who lost interest in jobs regardless of rewards, accolades or previous commitments to stay the course, when her work ceased to stimulate or excite her. J is exceptionally bright, an entrepreneur and a high achiever, but she knew that professionally she stood in her own way. J suspected that lurking behind her need for constant stimulation was an avoidance of commitment to both goals and intimacy.

J linked other development issues to her avoidance of tedium. Rather than merely skim the surface of her work projects, she wanted to pay greater attention to details. J longed to take time, stop rushing herself along. When she heard about Positive Structuring, she was immediately interested. She took notes on the three broad, essential steps in the process (determine the goal; research it; design a study model) and eagerly began her first Positive Structuring project by entering into the spirit of her chosen qualities. First, she spent several days listing words that exactly described the characteristics she wanted to cultivate. *Calm, clear-minded, tenacious, fluid, unmoved, peaceful* were all words that J related to. Words and our dictionary play significant roles in Positive Structuring. Words can be our first inroads to structuring an architecture of understanding. This scaffolding is built in our consciousness as we find our way to the concepts, images, behaviors, attitudes or products that best suit our Positive Structuring purposes.

---

*J represents a composite of several people.

Phase II: Exploration

In a week or so, having exhausted this first phase, J moved on to her Phase II tasks. Now she tried to generate specific, comprehensive details of the tenacity she wanted. J selected pictures of various craftspersons at work, each of whom demonstrated these characteristics. Painstakingly, she pasted photos of Japanese flower-arrangers as they assembled cut flowers into displays that seemed fully alive. She gathered advertisements that featured quiet work spaces that encouraged reflective, serious effort. In a journal, J grouped together an entire section of symbols that conveyed high-quality workmanship to her: logos of top-of-the-line pens, cars and foods whose very name conveyed integrity, superiority and meticulousness.

Phase III: Solution "Architecture"

As J entered Positive Structuring's third phase, she grew confused and sullen, even resentful. The entire invention process—the ideas and forms that had been ever present in her mind—slipped away from her. Now even this gifted person fumbled. She wanted help, but realized that for her own sake she had to author her own Phase III study model. Knowing this made her even edgier. Pushed to the wall of her self-imposed limits, her self-styled pattern of withdrawal and hostility, J realized she was up against the very traits that stymied her on the job and that others had problems with. She wanted to cultivate the exact qualities she denied herself. J could never have what she wanted if she resisted the final phase of this assignment. To paraphrase Pogo, the popular cartoon character, J met her enemy when she met herself.

J knew she was stuck and grew increasingly enraged. She was not bored, but would have to delve beneath the surface of the task to succeed. In other words, to satisfy the requirements of this task, J had to *do* the very thing she didn't want to do. If she quit this time, J knew she might never overcome the barrier that she herself had constructed to keep her talents at bay. If she chose to meet Phase III's inherent demands, she would soon grow beyond her self-limiting behaviors. She had no one else to blame.

J realized she could design (and learn from) almost any study model:

- *experiential,* taking actions that cultivate most-needed attributes;
- *physical,* such as building something tangible, producing a play or a home video; or
- *artistic,** such as creating sculpture, art or composing music that might embody the essence of her intention, or designing rooms emblematic of the reality she wanted.

In another month or two, an elated J phoned me. She had found an experiential Phase III model through which to structure her wished-for solution. She had enrolled in an aikido course. By signing up in the martial arts program, J confronted every avoidance that she'd perfected over a lifetime of resistance. Persevering through the pain, boredom, inconvenience and frustration of the discipline, J eventually taught herself how to stick with any task. Her experiential solution richly represented the heart and spirit of those several characteristics that she instinctively recognized she needed for self-development.

POSITIVE STRUCTURING AS CHILD'S PLAY

When we remember that as children we used play to pretend our way into complex learnings and competencies, we realize that recreation is a constructive, quite natural problem-solving mode—it is our heritage for achievement and personal development.

The route by which adults grow involves creative, rather than mechanical, processes. Fundamental to our personal effectiveness is mastery of those things we do best and that fascinate us. Yet each of us reaches plateaus—even in those things over which we have authority and control. We can enhance our dynamism by reminding ourselves how we learned as children and replicating that process. It is largely through a meandering play that we locate alternate routes when our way in the world is blocked. During relaxed, daydreaming or transitory times—moments or hours spent away from "work"—intuitive intelligence augments our verbal-analytical mind and gives us a chance for whole-seeing.

---

*"Physical" and "artistic" representations can be combined, although it may help some readers to think of these separately.

Even before we began school, we absorbed massive amounts of information and mastered several highly complex skills. We did so on our own. All healthy children instinctively express themselves—in their cribs, without parental aid or words. In time, without formal instruction, they learn to speak, to walk and to manipulate their environment.

Children are inherently creative constructionists, learning independently by building intellectual and physical structures. (Papert, 1980) Each child makes enormous developmental strides through everyday play. While parents ooh and aah as they watch their infants amuse themselves with their feet, toys or food, their babies are teaching themselves about spatial realities and learning what is and what is not their body. They are discovering new worlds: learning about themselves, about others and about what sort of restrictions, permissions, roles and perceptual patterns are appropriate in the context and reality into which they have been born. (Yamamoto, 1972) Children's play is hardly frivolous.

The child is instinctively an effortless, spontaneous player. Through imagination, using materials found at home, in their cribs or on floors, children instantly enter fictional worlds. These worlds, their own minds, are teachers. A child never questions "how" to pretend. The broom transports—a magic vehicle for conveyance; a cloud becomes a face or an elephant; bath towels are arranged into ball gowns. The five-year-old is twenty-five. Through play, nonconscious and free-associative abilities turn things that are into what they are not. In the process, children learn how to be, do and live in the drama of consensus reality that adults and culture have devised. Their recreation allows them to expand intellectually and to imagine the unimaginable—to be whatever they wish.

Some children receive richer materials and greater encouragement and have more opulent environments for their play. (Papert, 1980, p. 7) These speed and reinforce learning and enhance their construction capabilities. Adults, schooled away from their natural inclination to explore, are often crippled players, wooden and self-conscious. Their days of self-instruction are numbered. Worse, they cannot imagine themselves free of problems anymore. Perhaps one cause for this imprisonment is that adults cannot imagine and no longer play.

THE TYRANNY OF "ADULT" LOGIC

We warn ourselves to be logical. We limit our own mind—tell it not to dwell on the impossible. Life-predicaments are believed to be insolvable. As soon as we try to move even a small hill, disbelief and doubt magnify it into a huge mountain, and we are stymied. We find it unthinkable that future generations might live in space, underwater or on other planets; impossible to think of our body as healthy, as victorious over a disease or over the sorrow of a broken heart. Almost everyone has personal knowledge of a family member who thwarted his or her life because that person could not imagine being free of a limitation, an illness or shame. These seemed hopeless burdens.

Our enrollment in the School of Impossibles starts at birth. Sometimes our teachers are those who love us most. Our first lessons quite certainly involve memorizing what and what not to do at all times and in all places and situations. Our list of don'ts becomes so dense and weighty that eventually, like a lid, it closes our minds; many refuse from then on to open their thinking again.

Soon almost all of us stop playing for fun. We teach ourselves to approach everything, even recreational pursuits, in deadly earnest. We can't enjoy ourselves or others. We deify winning, rules and overcontrol. If, for example, we fumble while playing a game, we feel ashamed or get angry at ourselves. If others are slow, clumsy, forgetful or inept—or worse, if their wins exceed ours—we grow rude, irritable or self-critical. Sports or board games intended to be relaxing, insignificant, amusing diversion—simple conversation capable of building bridges of friendship toward others—become ulcer farms.

RELEARNING TO PLAY

Those who can still play with self-abandon, who can put their whole bodies and minds into an activity, rid themselves of tension. Time, space, and self-consciousness evaporate. Through play, whatever their ages, people expand, gain insight, skill and "see" pictures of what's possible. Imagination is still their trusted servant, a friend, as in childhood. These individuals routinely wonder and dream—are able to consider unthinkable things. What is still invisible becomes real. By freely pretending, the unimaginable becomes imaginable.

When we play—that is, when we stop trying, competing, comparing, intellectualizing, criticizing, judging and brutalizing ourselves and others—we rekindle true creativity. Certain key rudimentary mental functions spawn insights in the very area to which our work or playtime is committed.

Rollo May suggests that our mind's struggle, if properly intense and absorbed with its inquiry, *invites* the unconscious to answer with a complete pattern or gestalt. Our devoted search for answers signals to our nonconscious realm that an unfinished puzzle—an incomplete gestalt—exists. Then, over time, a breakthrough occurs—usually, to paraphrase May, when we put away books, go for walks, relax and take our mind away from its "work". (May, 1975, p. 66)

Through play, delight and self-forgetting, we see differently. We penetrate the heart of our chosen projects or games in a way that initiates us into the world of patterns, order and metadesigns. We discover the underlying principles or the randomness and chance that command respect and attention. (Yamamoto, 1972)

PHASE III STUDY MODELS: SITUATIONAL PLAY

Positive Structuring's magic and potential is also situational; we selectively extend relevant intellectual or behavioral skills. Since we carefully design and choose the circumstances of our study models, we stretch ourselves, expand the boundaries of our abilities and our personal universe in our greatest area of need. Through self-selected, strategically planned play, we explore the wilderness of the study model and in so doing look into the darkness of our own unknown. As we try to understand what our play is teaching us, we begin to draw our own conclusions about ourselves and the world. John Muir's remark, "The clearest way into the Universe is through a forest wilderness," now applies to us.

Every Phase III study model contains its own hinterland, which, when approached with quiet intelligence, leads us to some universal truth about whatever it is we seek.

These projects vary. Almost everything can be used productively—depending on our objective. We can sell something—anything: Tupperware, cosmetics, lemonade, car wax—and find an entrepreneurial microcosm. If we experiment with birding or nature hikes, we teach ourselves "how" to gain inner peace. If we take chess lessons, we discover "how" to improve concentration, strategic thinking. Or we might use chess as a way to practice the art of keeping our own counsel. If we are anxious, timid, self-conscious individuals, public speaking courses have much to offer. Remodeling and repair projects carry their own lessons, as do cooking classes, putting boats into bottles or sculpture. Our study model can involve things we currently enjoy. As a drop of water is, in small measure, exactly like what flows from the ocean or the tap—our study model holds a nucleus of our solution's realities when we create its metaphorical structure and relate these correspondences to our objectives. Because Positive Structuring introduces us to our own awareness, it delivers the ways and means for personal growth, higher consciousness and real-world effectiveness. As we do, we learn "how."

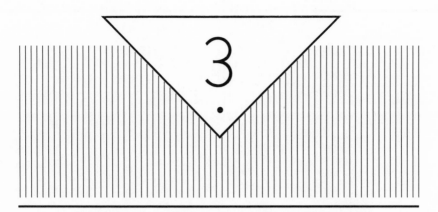

A 21st-CENTURY MIND INCUBATES SOLUTIONS

As far as incubation is concerned, it is a well-known fact—even in simple learning—that a process of consolidation is necessary. For instance, students know that they cannot well retain what they have learned just before taking a test. . . . They must "sleep on" the material. It could be that the material to be committed to memory must reverberate in the neuronal circuits, completely outside of consciousness, in order to make lasting connections.

SILVANO ARIETI, *Creativity*

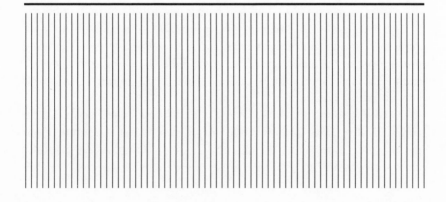

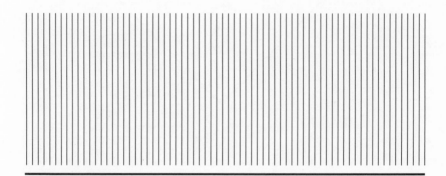

In *Living Happily Ever After,* I emphasized that we must believe ourselves capable of actualizing goals before they can be accomplished. Since Positive Structuring combines visualization and ongoing, active, absorbed engagement with desirable solutions, we eventually generate feelings of the thing we want as well as pragmatically structure a conscious design of the solution in our mind. We see it as possible for us, but only if we grasp the symbolic linkage between our "play" and our solution. We shift our consciousness toward our hoped-for answers and create the belief that these are attainable for us. Once this shift occurs, the goal is ours.

We design study models as microcosmic conceptions or mini-architectures of our solutions. For this reason, our clarity at the start is essential, since we don't have enough information for clarity in the beginning, the graduating preparatory steps taken before creating a model are completely necessary. It is natural to be impatient to get to the study models, thinking we can rush through the other steps. But urgency is counterproductive, since the unfolding process holds information that we need. Even I, who invented this method, cannot immediately come up with my own study models, although I can dream up dozens for someone else. The fact is that *our* problem holds subterranean messages for us. These messages are hidden in each of our nonconscious minds, and only we can access this. Usually understanding our inmost selves takes time. There is a Tibetan saying that my good friend Michael Toms likes to quote: "If we try to go quick, quick, we end up going slow, slow."

Initially, growth in skills, attitudes and knowledge begins almost automatically, as we sustain active imagination. Later we simulate our personal development by the practical model building. As we playfully construct physical or experiential representations, we become as children again and recapture our ability to use our minds as they were designed to be used: to help us grow, learn, gain mastery and create. In some unexplicable fashion, the answers we ultimately get are answers our various intelligences invent.

POSITIVE STRUCTURING DEVELOPS INCUBATION SKILL AND CREATIVE ADAPTIVITY

Positive Structuring is a concrete model-building method. It is experimental, noncompetitive and idiosyncratic. The study models are symbolic representations of our solutions or goals that over time produce a complete gestalt. (May, 1975, p. 66) To the extent we inject our imaginative powers into our design and model-building process, to the degree we are willing to proceed mindfully and conservatively, we construct potentially complex solutions. Then, too, we transfer our learnings. What we glean from our study model we carry over to more serious real-life dilemmas. While we bring specificity and symbolic shape or form to what is still intangible, like our dreams, or the as-yet untapped solutions we now hold unconsciously, we structure understanding and higher creative processes into our way of being.*

---

*Authors Lakoff and Johnson (1980) treat this matter of whole-seeing linguistically. They provide this helpful example of cause-and-effect learning that occurs through direct manipulation: "Our successful functioning in the world involves the application of the concept of causation to ever new domains of activity—through intention, planning, drawing inferences, etc." (p. 71) Through our proper grasp of causation, we begin to experience objects and activities as a gestalt, as a whole. (Piaget's hypothesis that infants initially discover causation by manipulating their blankets, spoons, food, etc., reinforces this idea.) My sense is that our consciousness evolves, unfolds, is enhanced by our physical play or manipulations. This evolution enables us to perceive wholistically, to penetrate the unitive nature of a matter. Thus, problem-solving ability, including causation insight, becomes enlarged as well.

POSITIVE STRUCTURING FOR THE CREATIVE
ADAPTIVE RESPONSE

A Sample Exercise—Phase I: Discovering "What"

At this point, I outline the course a positive structuring task follows from start to finish so we can have a clear idea of the steps involved. Along the way, we'll also get a clearer idea of what the creative adaptive response is. (In Chapter 4, I describe in greater detail how I have designed and implement an evolving, slow-to-unfold project.)

Suppose, for now, we want to use these techniques to strengthen our creative adaptive response. Perhaps we notice a decline in our successes, have lost confidence, and grow unhealthfully self-conscious or timid with each passing day. At work, at home, with our friends, we are increasingly insecure. By deciding to cultivate the three synergistic skills—positive self-valuation; autonomy; learning resourcefulness— we satisfy the first requirement of Positive Structuring: decide what we want to be, do or have. In Phase II, we immerse ourselves in the spirit of what it is we want—in this case, greater creative adaptivity.

Phase II: Research—Plumbing the Depths

Now we read, study or simply observe the desired skills cluster in a variety of ways. We find and observe admirable role models whom we imagine are creatively adaptive. Or, we create book lists and accumulate articles on this theme. Eventually, we read them. At this stage, our only job is to study and understand progressively more subtle layers of creative adaptivity as these nuances apply to our life. We never strain to adopt these traits or worry about "how" we will change. We merely observe the "what" with acute interest and objective absorption. In other words, we get involved mentally in the area we want creative adaptive applicability. A socially rigid person who hopes to be a spontaneously gracious, resourceful host might study Martha Stewart's flawless PBS program or read her books. Another, whose goal is to become a best-selling author, might adopt any number of standard observation exercises designed to improve a writer's craft: read fine

writers; rewrite outstanding poetry or prose pieces; improve vocabulary, etc. The aspiring creative host can increase his or her options by
packing beautiful lunches for the family. A physical project for someone aspiring to craftsmanship in any field might be raising bonsai trees,
since these miniature plants must be continually shaped into a sort of
living sculpture, and by doing this we learn about patience, proportion
and form. These skills can then be leveraged into greater use in our
actual craft or vocation. John Gardner's advice to writers sounds much
like what I am getting at here for everyone: "What one has to get, one
way or another, is insight—not just knowledge. . . . What one needs
is not the facts but the 'feel' [of the thing]" (Gardner, 1985 p. 31) If we
want greater creative adaptivity at work, we try to get the "feel of the
thing" in a narrow, low-risk area—we organize our desk; we use our
free time or practice at home. We do not experiment wildly when we're
throwing an important party or making a presentation in the board-
room.

Phase III: Solution Architecture—Creating a Model

Third, we plan an initial construction or study model building project.
Our job now is to create in an prototypical, small-scale replica the
experience of what we want. Our study model should embody or
somehow draw out of us the three synergistic attributes we want to
learn* (in this hypothetical case).

The would-be gracious host could practice entertaining for ordinary
dinner meals. The budding author might keep a minirecorder to track
interesting conversations. Let us say at first we decide to create an
experiential model to teach ourselves about independence, self-respect
and learning resourcefulness. We may feel totally frustrated by the
vague or elusive nature of this task. We wait for an idea. While blocked,
we must rest assured that all through this method, we are making
progress. We are, while waiting, incubating answers—even though
these don't surface immediately. Since we are required to think for
ourselves and to come up with our own project designs, we experience
exactly what artists, scientists and entrepreneurs do when they invent,
create or build something without fully knowing "how" to do it.

The process of Positive Structuring is a self-teaching vehicle for our

---

*Keep in mind that almost any goal can be substituted for the one under discussion.

creative adaptive response—no matter what other goal we want to learn or structure. As long as we remain engaged, absorbed or fascinated by a hard-to-grasp solution, this method instills creative thinking in us. Since we are compelled to struggle with an "incomplete gestalt,"* we are obliged to instruct ourselves in the essentials of flexible problem-solving and thus we become apprentice inventors. The greater our absorption with the study model, the likelier it is that we can break through to envision those projects that will teach us precisely what we need to know. The old saying "When you are ready, your teacher will appear" applies here. The appropriate study model is our guru.

At long last, a project springs to mind. Perhaps in seeking greater independence, we choose to reactivate a long-standing but discarded interest—take up a hobby that others have minimized and scorned. Or we decide to learn a new language, square dancing or basket-weaving. Perhaps we enroll in a craft class, say glass-blowing. Or, we can build an environment—out of balsa wood or on our computer. The instant we undertake any venture that, while personally fulfilling, also invites skepticism, criticism or rejection, our growth toward autonomy begins. Only independent souls are rich enough to afford the costs and luxury of identifying what they truly want and then moving boldly toward it.

We soon realize at some deep level that the longer we persevere with this new hobby, dance or language, the more we strengthen our autonomy. Now our lessons in resourcefulness begin, too. Attempting anything new introduces us to ourselves as learners. We observe anew our own discovery process, our preferences and strengths. Immersed in novelty, we build confidence in our ability to comprehend and master ourselves despite awkwardness or unsureness.

The synergistic skills cluster is not packaged neatly into three sleek boxes, or demarcated by sharp lines. We do not systematically graduate from one skill into the next. Rather, we concurrently strengthen all three major clusters. We regress, advance, stop to rest, regress again, advance some more, while enjoyably immersing ourselves in safe, sensible study models, embryonic to our goal.

---

*In describing the characteristics of his own creative process, Rollo May states, "One can quite accurately speak of this incomplete Gestalt, this unfinished pattern, this unformed form, as constituting 'the call' that was answered by the unconscious." (P. 66)

LOOSENING UP OUR MIND-SET—LEARNING TO "MESS AROUND"

As we practice Positive Structuring, we eventually loosen our too-fixed manner of responding. As I have said, this happens mysteriously. We work out new options in our daily life, add to and alter our usual way of seeing things, and thus stack the deck of solutions in our favor. We learn to organize ourselves around challenges we can handle by creating replicas, models and representations of them. However puny these models, they dictate to us, make us think and behave in novel ways. To solve the problems we choose to take on, we must communicate with ourselves in a deep, intensely intimate fashion—just as all artists, craftspersons or inventors do. This enhanced interior rapport builds external acumen.

Howard Rheingold's humorous look at untranslatable words in his book *They Have a Word for It* presents the term *bricoleur* for one who constructs things by "random messing around without following an explicit plan." This French term was apparently coined by anthropologist Claude Lévi-Strauss to describe the way "primitive" cultures approach learning theory. *Bricoleur* is defined as *"a kind of intuitive technician who plays with concepts and objects in order to learn about them"* (italics in original). (Rheingold, 1988, p. 90)

Computer scientist and co-creator of Logo (a computer language for children), Seymour Papert describes how the concept of *bricoleur* applies to thinking. Papert's idea is that as any of us—child or adult—work with what we've got, our tinkering lets us manipulate the building blocks in front of us. In addition, our play or random messing around also promotes deeper, nonconscious mental activity. In his book *Mindstorms,* he describes how his own play taught him to think along abstract, enhanced lines:

Before I was two years old I had developed an intense involvement with automobiles. The names of car parts made up a very substantial portion of my vocabulary: I was particularly proud of knowing about the parts of the transmission system, the gear box, and most especially the differential. It was, of course, many years later before I understood how gears worked; but once I did, playing with gears became a favorite pastime. I loved rotating circular objects against one another in gearlike motions and, naturally, my first "erector set" was a crude gear system.

I became adept at turning wheels in my head and at making chains of cause and effect: "This one turns this way so that must turn that way so . . ." Gears, serving as models, carry many otherwise abstract ideas into my head. (Papert, p. vi)

In other words, we, too, can learn to tinker with what might be our too-rigid mind-set. This in itself seems a 21st-century skill.

Physical building blocks as well as experiential ones help us grow. A friend of mine—a gifted artist—told me she was at her wit's end because her art was producing no income. She made up her mind to have one last art show and then—if necessary—quit. She consciously designed a "letting go" project during the months before the art show that amounted to a Positive Structuring model, although we had never discussed this method:

I had decided that if I was to be an artist, I needed at least enough income to support myself wholesomely. I was sick and tired of scrimping. For weeks before my show I practiced "letting go."

I consciously used every day to release my hold on art as a career and to seek direction for what I should do. I prayed. I wrapped each piece of art carefully, knowing that if it didn't sell, I would give it away. I used the time to imagine myself empty of ambition and ego, to become willing to do whatever God's will presented next. I entered my art show with as much desireless purity and innocence as I could muster.

To my great surprise, everything sold. Orders for artwork poured in. I had prepared myself for the worst, and the message I got was: Don't quit. Keep on going. I'm not sure "how" the previous weeks' preparation helped me clarify my vocation, but I am certain that it worked.

Rheingold suggests that when others laugh at our disorganized manner of approaching a problem, we tell them that we are just *bricoleurs*. Of course, I think all *bricoleurs* are just Positive Structurists at heart.

Positive Structuring also lets us express appreciation for our core self. The absorbed state that we must adopt for this method integrates, permits fusion, resolves opposites, intensifies confidence. We feel positive, feel new appreciation for our hidden self. As we attend to our own insights and acknowledge ourselves as capable creators, we come to see ourselves as properly and fully utilized persons. Our nonconscious responds in kind: As we rely on its resources, it rewards us with an incredible array of answers, options and real-world opportunities.

PRUDENT RISK-TAKING

Many of us let ourselves be manipulated into an undesirable, hemmed-in, restricted future. Positive Structuring can suggest ways out, but we must be willing to take some small risk. Sometimes our first steps show us Positive Structuring is not enough. It leads us to deeper learnings.

I am reminded of a client who wanted a divorce, but each time he confronted his wife, he ended up agreeing to have another child instead. He knew his wife manipulated him and held him in bondage in a loveless marriage through guilt and his love of his children; he also suspected that he himself elected to father another child. Thus, he restricted himself, set things up to limit his options. He lacked experience in dealing with all the tough demands of his life. In this major problem area, he was impotent. Only after taking a few low-risk steps toward his goal of speaking frankly with his wife did he realize the extent of his victim's mind-set. Passivity ruled his life. But it was more than merely a communication issue. In work, marriage and social life, he accommodated others. His marital problem was just the most obvious, painful symptom of a wholly misdirected life. His first model was simply to identify all those unsatisfying social engagements and volunteer committees to which he'd promised time. Next, one by one, he resigned from these. Since growth accompanies our first productive step in the area of need, every tangible result increased his motivation. His get-off-the-committees model showed him that he'd suppressed his impulse for life, even his sexuality, through an overriding need to please. He believed he could best undo such long-practiced docility through psychotherapy, and found a therapist who specialized in men's issues. Along with this he designed two Positive Structuring models: a nightly practice of recording his positive daily acts of assertion and monthly weekend retreats at a yoga and health center. The nightly listing was his way of registering progress; the monthly weekends built strength and body-awareness, which he sensed his powerlessness had blocked. Since his wife didn't go with him, the weekends were a way of testing himself, as an independent person, in an unfamiliar setting.

All these steps grounded his attention on his solutions, and, incrementally, he grew into a resourceful, self-governing individual. I mention
this circuitous example because we, too, may advance only in a roundabout way. Here is when others' productive, if indirect, patterns can
help us endure.

Often, when we discover that we cannot solve problems from our
existing vantage point, our resulting frustration leaves us depressed.
Then it is easy to turn viciously against ourselves, or against family and
society. The nightly news indicates many people do just this. Faced
with the need to adapt or change, those who are dependent, fearful, or
thwarted can become risk-averse, entrenched and even addicted to
hopelessness or their worst possible solutions. Chemicals, mind-numbing hours spent watching television, apathetic vegetating and endless
seeking for rescue from the latest quick-fix experts bring only the
illusion of safety, if that. In my corporate practice, I see numerous
examples of well-entrenched bureaucracies and individuals shooting
themselves in the feet to avoid finding their way out of difficulty.

Some people shy away from all risks. They blame their spouses,
managers, parents or society for their inability to act. Others are like
zombies: eerily inactive until specifically instructed how to do a thing.
The distressing truth is that few people expect themselves to be truly
resourceful—either at work or in their personal lives. Americans have
been among the most innovative people in the world, but recently we
seem to have lost our edge. Only those rare independent, self-trusting
souls whose minds shy away from mass-produced answers or robotic
responses still contribute to our national heritage of resourcefulness.

I recall hearing about a high school student who could solve every
algebraic equation in his head with complete accuracy, but he failed
algebra because he could not demonstrate to his teachers how he did
his calculations, nor could he learn the plodding theorems on which the
rest of his class relied. This is how we, too, are coaxed or prodded away
from our power. In order to be like, and be liked by, others, we use our
minds as others use theirs. We forfeit our creative thought processes
and our joy.

By contrast, the creative adaptive mind *learns* to use itself in whatever way works best and develops its own wholesome expansion. If you
do not feel you get the concept of Positive Structuring yet, rest assured
that each chapter contains several more sample exercises; each throws
more light on the entire subject. At this point, it seems sufficient to say
that it is not so important what models we design as it is that we
experiment with the progression, play at "figuring out." It's precisely

this tinkering, this noodling about with one idea or goal, that stretches thinking skill, helps us become objective observers of our minds, teaches us to hear our unique thought-language. Remember: "Figuring out" is a skill.

Although Positive Structuring is frustrating at first, soon it helps us activate our inherent inventive abilities. The more we dwell on our solutions, the more our attending habit can become a meditation lifting our thinking into new creative realms. It is this lift, this ongoing (if playful) focus, that eventually brings power.

There is an old Siberian folktale that says the young shaman must travel in spirit through a hole in the top of his head in order to penetrate the Highest Heaven:

> "Up above," gestures a shaman of the Tungus tribe, "there is a certain tree where the souls of the shamans are reared, before they attain their powers. And on the boughs of this tree are nests in which the souls lie and are attended. . . . The higher the nest in this tree, the stronger will the shaman be who is raised in it, the more will he know, the farther will he see." (Powell, 1982, p. 82)

Of course, there is no tree in our heads. Of course, we are neither shamans nor disciples of Siberian folktales. But our minds are capable of soaring. The process of discovery is one of its chief functions. Like young Siberian shamans, the higher up in our tree of consciousness we learn to go, the farther will we see.

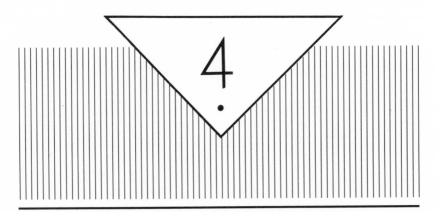

A 21st-CENTURY MIND IS LOGICALLY INTUITIVE

My beloved is the mountains, the solitary wooded valleys, strange islands . . . silent music.

SAINT JOHN OF THE CROSS

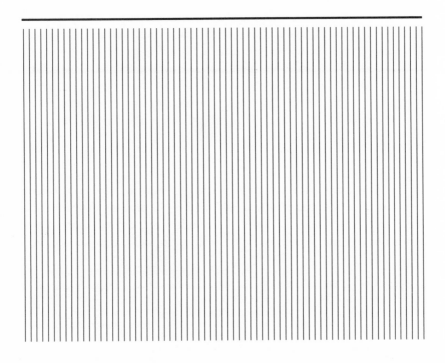

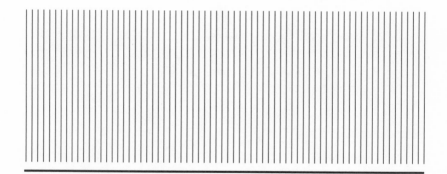

In general, creative adaptive people are not strangers to the experience of heightened consciousness. Their thoughts and actions often flow out of an unbounded awareness that I call "unitive." By no means do I suggest that simply because someone is creatively gifted he or she is fully enveloped in the unitive state.* True unitive consciousness, as described by theologians such as Martin Buber, is still rare. Buber relates unitive consciousness to an ecstatic, mystical union with God:

> What is experienced in ecstasy (if one may really speak of a "what") is the unity of the I. But in order to be experienced as unity, the I must have become a unity. Only one who is completely unified can receive unity. . . . Now the content of its experience and the subject of its experience, world and I, have flowed together. . . . Now one is removed from the commotion, removed into the most silent, speechless heavenly kingdom—removed even from language, which the commotion once laboriously created to be its messenger and handmaiden, and which [eternally desires] the impossible thing . . . truth, purity, poem. (Buber, 1985, p. 5)

I use the term unitive consciousness to describe a perceptual field, intuitive power and the functional blending of interior/exterior realities. These faculties could not and would not exist without unitive influence. I hope to demystify the notion, to include larger numbers

---

*I am not ignoring theological ramifications, nor forgetting facts: only a fortunate few are graced by goodly measures of unitive consciousness. Still, I say that the seeds of unitive consciousness *influence* many more people than we imagine—especially those who are growing autonomous, who possess increasing stores of positive valuation, exhibit learning resourcefulness and embody the Being values—all attributes of both unitive consciousness and the psychosociology of creative adaptation.

and types of people. My sense is that therapy, self-help books and "experts" can do little to open us up to the unitive state, although these may sensitize and help ready us for whatever is deepest within. On the other hand, prayer, meditations, certain arts and physical disciplines, music and a host of esoteric and traditionally spiritual practices quite easily move us into this inner world in terms of direct experience.

CREATIVE ADAPTIVE OPENNESS

Well-developed creative adaptives are typically open to their nonconscious functions. They experience being fully alive almost all the time. They attend inwardly, yet are superbly connected to reality and possess sound "reading skills"—interpretive acuity, an ability to read subtle personal, interpersonal and environmental cues. Not only do interior images, intuition and values prompt their spontaneous and self-disciplined choices, but they also merge these most complex insights with the concrete demands of their life, often with surprising success. This uniting of objective and subjective permits the full flowering of their self-expression.

Perhaps more important, creative people see "nonordinarily." As a general rule, the greater their psychological health, the more discerning, accurate and whole their perception of reality. The *process* of their life-choices, thinking and acts seems more like dance than like a mechanistic, militaristic march. Self-trust plays an important part in their intuitive dance—a factor that again underscores their ability to meet change with fewer formulas than the rest of the population. A gifted young teacher told me, "I don't want to live by prescriptions. Life *is* change, and too lovely to try to run it like a machine."

Inflexible people often believe themselves to be controlled by others or by external events and circumstances. This is one reason such individuals are themselves intensely controlling, strive to work harder or woodenly manage self or others. Such individuals believe they lack choices and generally feel trapped. For instance, Americans currently face the loss of leisure time. Recent polls show us working longer hours than twenty years ago, while our Western European counterparts somehow work less than in the past. We say leisure time—not work, not money—is our chief ambition, and we seek ways to add free time to our lives. (Naisbitt, 1990, pp. 1–3) My observation tells me that working "smarter"—e.g., living by our own prescriptions of what's relevant; not trying to run our life like a machine—is the answer. Yet only a creatively adaptive mind thinks like this, is receptive to the nuances and choices of nonrobotic living and willing (when it's necessary to health, family or spirit) to cut back on luxuries or to simplify work along the lines I have described elsewhere. (Sinetar, 1987)

Creative adaptives are also more open than others to their entire experience, including the unknown and nonordinary consciousness, their dream-fantasy life and darkness—fears, negative emotions, tensions, injustice. From this, they synthesize and construct elements of reality, solutions or ways of being that others tend to ignore, suppress or discount. Annie Dillard comments, "Appealing workplaces are to be avoided. One wants a room with no view, so imagination can meet memory in the dark." (Dillard, 1989, p. 6) Her words express the sentiments of many highly creative people: darkness and the unknown feed and stimulate their genius—not their fears.

Simply because people are creatively adaptive does not mean they are necessarily geniuses. Rather, they have reached an elevated level of functioning and are supported by the powers of their own raised consciousness. The Buddhist saying "If you want the truth, just see what your original face was—before you were born" expresses this point. Yet the fact that many people manage to ignore the obstacles, prejudices and superstitions that the majority culture has traditionally placed in the way of creative adaptive expressions may make them supernormal.

FINDING STRENGTH THROUGH NONDOING

A "no-formula" life can temporarily confound even those who habitually try to live it. I recently heard about a middle-aged man whose graduate-school advisers told him that he would never succeed in the entertainment field. His professors thought him too old, inexperienced and poorly prepared and warned him away from even trying.

Crestfallen, he seriously considered quitting, but part of him stubbornly refused to believe he couldn't make it. This persistent life-pulse was his first and primary inner note of hope. He took a short vacation—altered his usual schedule, and did whatever helped him amplify this inaudible yet persistent inner message. He spent time alone, meditated and "just puttered." He designed his weekend as a solitary retreat, listened to music and visited museums. "I needed to be immersed in those moods and images that encourage my deepest purposes. I wanted reminders of my values. For a while my professors' words had erased these from my mind. I heard their warnings, but not my own wishes."

One day he was caught by a single thought: In an obstinate way, he thoroughly enjoyed the challenge of pitting himself against the opinion of those who said he "couldn't make it." He sensed that this enjoyment provided the very endurance and energy required for success. He gave himself permission to continue and began lining up job interviews. Within two months, he obtained an entry-level position at a major network, where he is now building the career he wants.

This example serves us because it shows that normal people spot times, or phases, in their decision making when nondoing is appropriate. Then they watch or listen inwardly. A computer scientist friend calls this a "fuzzy feeling" period where he is so unclear about what to do that trying to act is futile. Another friend says when she doesn't know what to do she "holds" her intentions gently and in time her problem resolves itself. I recently heard one man say this technique never fails. "I sit alone and quietly, with my eyes closed. I put aside all my concerns about the problem. My only aim is to know the truth and to be willing to act on it when it arrives. That's all. Then I wait. Within minutes or days I get a hunch or a flash of insight. That's all it takes." It is primarily the psychologically healthy person who waits, in nondoing fashion for intuition's cues while gently observing complex, contradictory sets of feelings, goals and external circumstances.

IDEAS NEED TIME TO INCUBATE

Positive Structuring lets us use rest periods or regressions to take time to explore our true motives, interior and external realities. During this phase, we probe our darkness; we try to see and feel our way intuitively.

What begins in confusion, anarchy and often anxious, fearful dread evolves into intensely creative results. As we wait and watch, enduring the sometimes painful fact that we don't know what to do and don't know which way to go, we give ourselves fully to the depths and mysteries of consciousness. This passive waiting, this nondoing, seems our message to ourselves saying we trust our answers will come. Our assuredness and faith transmit a signal to our core that we have sacrificed fully to the directives of its power.

If we open up in this nondoing fashion, while simultaneously asking ourselves the questions "What am I to do? How shall I go?," this amounts to a silent—if, for many, secular—prayer. In fact, this is a prayer, whether we like the term or not, and it indicates we are consciously struggling with an "incomplete gestalt." We alternately meditate on our questions and let go. In direct proportion to the degree of purity, innocence, faithful and positive expectancy with which we ask, we are answered. Instead of being fatigued or made hopeless by our waiting, we now find ourselves renewed and hopeful—and especially if our intense search is complemented by relaxed play.*

This hiatus is a most useful phase, with rich potential for detached observation and idea incubation. During this reflective, ambiguous period, some people think, learn or daydream in predominantly visual images, even in colors. Others use their own physicality and movement: They walk, dance, pace or practice some routinely ordinary task (wash a floor, clean out the garage) or they select a physical discipline (yoga, swimming or running, etc.) to help them think. During such a workout, ideas and answers pop up from nonconscious realms of awareness. Still others use sound (music, interior mental "conversation," the sound of water, etc.) to entice or stimulate the hunches they hope to receive. Or they combine modalities.

Images, ideas or answers are often triggered by illogical or irrational means—not by linear, intellectual methods. Some of my best ideas come to me while I'm walking or driving in the country, thinking about nature or the rural architecture, and I recently discovered a precursor to this idea-generating stage.

My long walks or drives are actually the final stage in an extended process. Months before, I clean out cupboards, shelves, files, my garage. The more serious the issues I'm incubating, the greater the emptying: Old homes are sold, and I move to new ones. Clothes, files, books— anything and everything—goes. Lesser concerns find me throwing out lesser things or establishing fresh routines and rituals in relatively unimportant areas of my life. When I speak of this during lectures, amazing numbers of people report they do the same thing. As one audience member put it, "It's as if my psyche needs more space, grows through this emptying, this movement—whatever that happens to be. If I don't take this time, I block personal growth and my most creative insights."

---

*I have written elsewhere, and frequently, that love, "higher" consciousness and positive, productive energy seem one and the same. We are energized, alive and joyful as we focus on, love or devotedly approach the object of our inquiry. The whole universe extends itself to us as we extend ourselves to it in this way, since these elements are the stuff of the cosmos, the ties that bind and connect us universally.

I rarely know why I'm cleaning cupboards or taking long drives but now rest assured that a higher logic rules this intuitive, organic activity.

STIMULATING INTUITION: POWER TASKS

Many activities produce such rich personal insight that they might be thought of as power tasks. They empower us. They stimulate intuition and afford lasting, productive growth. In general, when our acts promote self-awareness, hunches and healthy behaviors, we can think of them as our favored power tasks. For example:

- Reading, thinking intensely—absorption in specific problems, goals or topics activates unconscious processes and self-awareness;
- Self-observation—strong feeling, even an overreaction, often triggers important awarenesses;
- Dreaming and dream therapies—vibrant, meaningful dreams (especially those that repeat or leave lasting impressions) are doors to the unconscious;
- Silent modes of self-exploration—meditation, journal-keeping, prayer, silent uninterrupted periods or solitude;
- Attending to personal symbols: myths, fairy tales, theater, art, music, nature, can all reveal elements, language and motifs we find charming, fascinating, threatening, "lucky," healing. There are messages here, even if only in our interpretation;
- Physical adventures—walking, selected personal disciplines, physical metaphors—encourage behavior changes and self-awareness, engage our thought processes in challenges and ongoing revelation.*

In Pat's case, described in Chapter 2, learning to draw with her left hand and engaging in interpretive dance produced enormous personal

---

*A friend of mine says fire-walking changed his life. Others report they have gained self-confidence and improved creativity by such programs as *Outward Bound,* the Pole Course and the Ropes Course, wherein people are pitted against themselves to find their own solutions. For anyone who feels fire-walking and wilderness trips are extreme, or who wonders if the solutions gained when using metaphors that someone else creates *for them* are as expanding as those a person creates for his/herself, Positive Structuring seems yet another alternative. With Positive Structuring, our mind must identify the goal, design the "course" of study and invent both the metaphorical structures by which to learn and find the answers in these constructs.

growth. Our preference might be to walk regularly in a favorite park or listen to a favorite piece of music. Whatever our chosen method for quickening self-awareness, we can be sure that as we dignify or respect our own unconscious processes, we will meet intuition's spirit. For instance, can we find a piece of music that "sounds like" our solutions or our goal? We may sense that our solution's "energy" or tone is lively, strong and quick-paced, while our usual, more dominant mood and tempo are slow and funereal. If this is the case, we may have the impulse to examine our plodding tendencies, see that this will never take us where we say we want to go. Before long we may find that we learn best when involved with a predictable group of activities or modes of thought. In their initial exploration of power tasks, some people automatically want to be in remote, pristine settings, while others gravitate to urban offerings. One friend always secretly yearned to go on an Outward Bound program, and finally gave herself permission to attend. Her wilderness experience was so liberating, promoted so much growth, confidence and self-awareness, that within a few months of completing the course she had reunited with her husband, found a better job and was planning to enroll in graduate school. Almost everyone can find rewarding projects or learning situations that awaken intuition.

Highly creative people usually are able to identify their preferred method for stimulating intuition. Others must first consciously observe themselves to find out just how and when to draw our their best ideas. Vera John-Steiner's overview of the habits and "thought-languages" of experienced thinkers underscores the multiple variables involved. She describes numerous avenues through which creative thinkers consciously incubate and then extract ideas from their nonconscious world. A majority rely on visual thought-symbols, while a few mix visual and kinesthetic images, as Einstein did. In one early "thought experiment," he combined a playful imaginary scene with his visualization of light-wave theory and "he imagined himself riding through space . . . astride a light wave and looking back at the wave next to him." (John-Steiner, 1987, p. 85)

A professor described his internal thought-symbols as a sort of anthropomorphic committee with whom he "meets" freely to stimulate both his visual and auditory functions:

Whenever I'm stuck, I just gather all my [mental symbols] together and have a conference with them. I've created these images to be liaisons to my unconscious. I tell them what I need and assign tasks to each one. Then I send them "out" to my unconscious to gather data for my solutions.

If they don't bring back what I need, then we have another little talk and I send them out again. In the long run, the answers that they bring me are amazing—I couldn't think them up in my usual way.

My own way is to build idea-structures just as architects design, then build, houses. I construct my conceptual framework in two ways. First, I draw the scaffolding, using a private, quite-incomprehensible written language of arrows, phrases, line drawings and, sometimes, numbers. (Some of these drawings are over a decade old—I keep adding to them, because even when my notes are undecipherable, I know something is happening underground.) On the surface, I can't easily trace my overall long-term creative process, so my scribbles are an invaluable personal shorthand. These let me communicate with my nonconscious and, apparently, enable translation of invisible, inexpressible concepts into visible forms and products. Darwin, Virginia Woolf, Martha Graham, Tchaikovsky and numerous others also condensed their ideas into drawings and notes that they stored and used in various ways. Notebooks, working blueprints or drawings and personal papers are all appropriate systems, as are letters and photographs. Each individual has his/her individual favorite codes.

I also employ tangible, hands-on construction projects to help me move ideas into reality and to express the evolvement of my own consciousness. For me, the plasticity of wood and wire corresponds with the plasticity of my mind. As I've said, Positive Structuring grew out of such play. If I can express my ideas in representational physical terms, it seems my learnings take on new depth.

VALUING CHOICES: THE ROLE OF POSITIVE SELF-VALUE

I am not suggesting that creative adaptives are antirational or that they disrespect their logical thought processes. By definition such persons tend to function effectively, using as much of their minds as they can and respecting their multiple intelligences—rational and nonrational. My interviews, personal experiences and professional observations suggest that those with heightened creative adaptive skill prioritize their intelligences, trust themselves to know which mind to use when. In almost every instance, they are temperamentally disposed to lean on and trust their own judgment rather than the advice of others. After completing a major project, an artist friend said, "I went through a monthlong torpor—I didn't know what was happening. All I could do was eat, sleep and stare out the window. Then, one morning, immediately on waking up, I knew it was over—I started to work in a most beautiful, disciplined way." People like this artist respect rather than fear their mysteries, look into their unknown, address their nonconscious, "speak" to their inmost secret core.

Returning to my early comments about positive self-valuation, self-trust distinguishes mature creative adaptives from those who are less developed. Many people with excellent creative potential tell me that they imagine, visualize, and write or draw their way to solutions. But the less secure somehow sap and undermine this available power. They apologize for their nondoing, find reasons that help them rationalize their use of asymmetrical, nonlinear problem-solving methods. For example, a person less confident than the professor quoted above might hide the fact that he consults with an internal "committee". Indeed, he could even consult a therapist to find out what is "wrong" with him for holding such internal dialogue. A friend of mine seems ashamed that she keeps a journal. She lists psychological "reasons" for wanting it to remain private. Another individual ridicules himself for using visualization techniques.

As self-trust increases, we start to legitimize and validate our own thinking-rituals and intellectual traditions, our feelings and hunches. We develop such tools to our advantage in whatever ways work best. Our positive self-regard lets us dignify our mind's native tongue. We begin to govern our minds instead of allowing our thoughts to rule us. In this governing lies one difference between high genius and madness.

Whether through hunches, dreams, "gut feelings" or other self-styled methods, creative adaptors believe in themselves sufficiently to court and honor their inner state. Their idiosyncratic song of life is largely an interior melody, leading them in a unique existential dance. In matters of health, relationship, values, religion or vocation, creative adaptives depend on instinctive wisdom as their primary guidance tool. As that clever book *The Tao Jones Averages* suggests, even financial profit can be gained by intuitive investing.

We are all intuitive (and can enhance our intuition) to the extent that we depend on our own insights, self-perceptions and intellectual processes.* A client comes to mind, a brilliant corporate strategist and an engineer. By training and temperament, he is a scientist. Methodical, logical, coolly rational and unemotional, his thought process seems chillingly linear to me. Yet he, too, personifies a creative adaptive approach to problem-solving. He consults and—more important—relies on his own special blend of intellect, intuition and instinct, even though he retains numerous highly paid advisers. I doubt that he makes decisions by taking long strolls in the park. Yet, impelled to struggle for and search out his own answers, he, too, trusts his own mind as his most reliable barometer for planning and action.

DREAMS CAN AND DO SERVE LIFE

Dreams have traditionally provided a major source of inspiration and direction for intuitive people. Scientists are familiar with the story of Friedrich August von Kekule, who, while dozing in front of his fireplace, dreamed of the structure of the organic compounds that were later to become a cornerstone of modern chemistry. (Goldberg, 1983) From where did his precise visualization and understanding come? How did he possess the details of a discovery that wouldn't be made until years later? Ordinary, less gifted persons also have such revelatory or prophetic dreams, and we cannot explain them, either.

Swiss psychiatrist Carl Jung researched and wrote extensively about the universal symbolism of dreams. (Jung, 1953, 1957, 1964) He concluded that a dream is the "hidden door" to our soul's innermost recesses that connects us to our egoless, whole self and to a cosmic, universal consciousness. In the deepest sense, our spontaneous development as persons can be enhanced and greatly furthered by our proper interpretation of the patterns and symbolism of our dreams. Just how this development is enhanced varies from individual to individual. Some experience a rush of energy and optimism when they correctly understand a dream series. Others gain specific life-supportive insights from a particular dream. The fact remains that dreams can and do serve life.

---

*If we don't have a dependable track record of good results when we've trusted our hunches or intuition, we should not begin by jumping into the deep waters on this. Unless, of course, we are particularly eager to lose all our money betting on a horse or a stock simply because a dream, gut feeling or tea-leaf reading tells us to proceed.

MANY PATHS LEAD TO INTUITION

No amount of skepticism from others dissuades creative adaptors from the conviction that they gain power, however fleeting, when attending to their intuition. As we have seen, creative people have their own favorite way of eliciting and hearing their inner cues as well as preferred rituals for drawing these out. Some meditate regularly, using classical or self-styled meditation methods. Others (and this seems especially true for men for obvious reasons) report that in the morning, while shaving or showering, useful ideas and salubrious planning directives come to mind. A friend keeps photos of the thing he wants on his desk. A few people warn against being too specific when talking about a favored method for tapping this inner landscape. Others freely disclose what works for them. Then, too, I have heard experts advocate strict goal-setting procedures for prompting intuitive ideas. One method asks us to write down a detailed description of what we need or want. Another is a formalized, playful self-questioning process that somehow is supposed to jog or stimulate the mind's flow of novel ideas. I find such questions irritating, but my own methods could irritate others as well. My experience is that almost any modality works to encourage our intuition if and when we believe in it, or if it has been effective previously.

In Chapter 2, I discussed a model for using Positive Structuring to increase creative adaptation generally. Now I suggest more detailed steps for designing a way to "grow" intuitive skills.

Phase I: Exploring Intuition

Approach any personal interest or concern as you might a formal research project, and plan to invest some time in the investigatory or "fuzzy" phase of your inquiry. Write out a question about your intuition on a piece of paper and just think about it. Take notes on your thoughts from as many sources as you can find: fiction, nonfiction, radio, television, books, magazines, lectures, dreams, conversations with others and so on. Soon you will notice that you listen and observe differently—with greater receptivity, acuity, vividness—in every area of life, but especially in your question or problem area. Increasingly, bits and fragments of data will seem to pop up from everywhere as parts of answers relating to your research. Write these ideas down. Honor them. In due time, your very vocabulary or way of speaking will become specifically helpful to the feelings or experience of intuition you want to capture. After a few weeks or months of totally immersing yourself in a specific area of inquiry, you'll begin having gut feelings about what you should do, read or buy.

Imagine (through visualization) or hear (through interiorized sounds) or feel (with your physical memory) what you want from intuition. Come at this *as if* you already had your goal. How would you be, act, feel, if you already possessed your answers or your objective? The metaphysician Neville once said, "Acceptance of the end wills the means to that end." This does not imply that we develop an old-fashioned, Victorian will of iron or force our way to our desired outcomes or use magical rituals to try to control nature or our own psyches. This never works. Rather, we intelligently align ourselves with our solutions or goals. We find ways to dance with our answers (or our question), attend to these inaudible yet distinctive vibrations. This beginning step of Positive Structuring can be an absorbing, lengthy period.

Clients who have adopted Positive Structuring—even those who never go beyond this initial "as if" step—tell me that the precise book they need, the exact one containing pertinent information for their field of inquiry, falls into their hands when they enter a bookstore. Or—on a hunch—they'll attend a lecture, meet a friend, or make a phone call, which then produces a lead to the specific information they want.* Many of us think of this as mere coincidence, but Carl Jung believed our psyche is a "door that opens on the human world from a world beyond." This mysterious world "allows unknown and mysterious powers to act upon [us]" and, if in faith we persist, answers do come. (Jung, 1953, p. 321) When logic fails us, we are often desperate enough to find our way using other means, whatever we may prefer to call these.

---

*Dr. Jean Bolin's book *The Tao of Psychology* helpfully discusses this phenomenon (termed synchronicity and originally detailed at length by Jung).

ADVANCED PHASES: USING DAILY LIFE FOR SELF-DISCOVERY

Earlier I wrote that architecture helped me grow. For almost a year, I have tried to remodel a tiny cabin in the Pacific Northwest. I bought it for logical reasons, all practical. It was a good investment. I wanted an office and business support system in the area, needed an airport close by. On the face of it, this was an easy, short-term remodel. But from the start it felt mysteriously unwieldy, and I was not willing to leave well enough alone.

After gutting the house, removing doors, floors, windows, counter-tops and the entire bathroom, I saw my quick-fix project deteriorate into a financial black hole, a bottomless money-pit.

During these months of remodeling delay, I repeatedly visited a small Japanese boutique in Seattle that sells old, museum-quality Japanese art. I bought things I can't possibly use in my present home. This behavior caught my attention. (When I say that we can each be artists, can use daily life to honor our goals, I mean that we can utilize all the means and materials at our disposal to understand the specific nature of our authenticity and intuitively "construct" our way to this.) Many things—e.g., behaviors and feelings—helped me identify the nature of my deepest objectives.

For instance, I became an avid overnight collector of ancient temple bells. Then, too, months passed and I was still remodeling, still pouring money into a 750-square-foot cottage. I buy costly, all-porcelain fix-tures and imported white tile for, by now, the all-new bathroom. I hire master carpenters to craft new transoms, floors, decks and French doors. I scout the finest antique shops, hunting for priceless leaded-glass windows. I forgo a vacation in Ireland so that I can have time just to sit in the cabin. With detached amusement, I watch all this, trying to catch on. "What," I ask myself, "is going on?"

About this time, a reader sends me a clipping from the *Houston Chronicle* describing a minimalist high-rise apartment of an architecture professor. (Cross, 1989) The article contains one blurry photo of a huge, uncluttered space. The massive unadorned room seems amaz-ingly intelligent and aesthetic. Something about its pristine mood stays with me. For the next few days, I think about other open-space envi-ronments: sacred buildings, selected museum rooms, even old barns. The vividness and rapidity of all this "new" data alerts me: I'm now receiving clues to my remodeling mystery. One night, while rereading

Frederick Buechner's book *Wishful Thinking,* his passage describing holy places grabs my attention. Buechner writes that places, people and things can all be holy when they have "God's mark" on them. His words capture the celestial essence of an old workshop. It has a wood-burning stove, a dark, dented workbench, a girlie calendar on the wall and smells of a mix of wood and pipe smoke:

> The windows are small and even on bright days what light there is comes through mainly in window-sized patches on the floor.
>
> I have no idea why this place is holy but you can tell it is the moment you set foot in it if you have an eye for that kind of thing. For reasons known only to God, it is one of the places he uses for sending his love to the world through. (Buechner, 1975, p. 39)

Buechner's clarity generates immediate insight: Ancient temple bells, Japanese art and sculpted gardens, restless meandering through antique shops and building-supply stores, an unfinishable remodeling project— all these bits fuse into whole-sight: I need to create a space that reflects unitive consciousness. My little cottage is simply a metaphorical arrow, pointing me toward clearer vision of my own inner state: I want a physical environment that speaks of the unseen, ineffable reality behind all materiality.

Alone, these bits of information mean little. Connected, they seem like a Baroque fugue, whose interlocked harmonies lead us rhythmically into coherent understandings. Once we identify our truest interior drives, then logic and our rational mind help move us along these lines.

This is how architectural projects can be indirectly helpful. But I advise others against this route unless they are already artists and thus understand the costs and penalties of this roundabout mode of operation. Most artists use experience, feelings and materials as tools. Their hobbies, money, houses, projects, problems, moods, conversations direct them, help them read their own truths. But impulsive Phase III starts are expensive. I choose to flow with mine because this is really my best way. However, I recommend the more methodical progression inherent in Positive Structuring's Phase I, II and III tasks. Jumping into the middle of things can be hazardous. This should be avoided unless we are particularly eager to squander time, energy, money and other valuables on "just" exploring. Or, unless this is our inherent play.

To me this exploration is "it"—wonderful fun. I enjoy it, love the ride and have found all investments worth it in the long run.

On a lesser scale of risk, we can become familiar with, then use, our flaws—even our small quirks—rather than fight, discount or hide these. When we go with the flow of our interior energies in smaller, safe ways, nothing is lost. No experience, "mistake," feeling, dream fragment, no past relationship, newspaper article (or scaled-down remodeling project) is for naught. We can, if we are of such a mind, consciously fold all experience into our awareness and examine it so that everything teaches us, becomes a readable message furthering our true life.* The spontaneity and appropriateness of this sort of "flow" is captured in a story about a Zen master invited to deliver an important speech. Just as he stands up, a bird sings. On hearing its song, he says, "The lecture has been given," and sits down. This behavioral flow gives witness to what Martin Buber calls a "silent, speechless kingdom," is truth, purity and poem in action.

THE SOMETIMES TRYING NATURE OF THE CREATIVE MIND

Personally, I work in an upside-down, inside-out fashion. As the last anecdote may reveal, I often start at the outer edges and move to the middle or center of things. This may mean I move backward from my desired outcome (or vision) toward the beginning steps that I must take. I enjoy and trust my own muddled way in this regard. Delays, impasses, bouts of sleepiness or hyperactivity seem necessary to my objective. This seems an organic process, and all these fluctuations of mood or habit count in the final analysis.

In some peevish, perverse manner, almost all successful creative adaptives that I interview feel and behave in a similar characteristic way: They refuse to give valuable time to paper shuffling, committees or busywork. Either through resistance, avoidance or outrightly declin-

---

*I don't suggest that we run with our killer-impulses, or rape, plunder and maim our way to our goals just because this seems the "flow" of our interiority. I am, after all, writing about and for (hopefully, God help me) psychologically healthy people for whom even inhibitions exist for good reason. (Frigidity and impotence come to mind as examples—perhaps these occur when one is with a loveless partner with whom it would be self-destructive to let go, or when one does not love oneself enough to tolerate pleasure.)

ing a project, they sense that in the long run certain prescribed or lockstep tasks defeat them. In whatever respects these individuals differ, they share one factor—they require freedom in, and control over, their vocational arena.

Catherine, a woman I interviewed in depth, told me that her former roommate used to urge her to make up a schedule of when she would and wouldn't be in town. The roommate wanted the schedule up to six months in advance, which of course Catherine could not have provided.

> I did my best but often didn't want to commit myself so far in advance. The fluidity of my life made my roommate very nervous, and she often inquired if I wouldn't be more comfortable with a "steadier" life.

Rollo May's poignant observation that dogmatists, bureaucrats and politicians cannot stand the "secret freedom" of creative people and processes reinforces my bias that creative adaptives are particularly adept at moving through and around external controls. John Gardner says that talented writers must possess a certain "stubbornness, even churlishness. . . ." I believe these qualities serve all of us when used with intelligence and proper timing, and keep us plodding along our own peculiar way. Unconsciously we may know that the usually free and bad advice others give us will be suicidal if followed. I have devoted pages (even full chapters) in my last books to the benefits of what I call positive rebellion, which sums up this issue more completely than is appropriate here.

One executive vice president throws out 80 percent of the forms and employee surveys her corporation requires managers to complete. The 20 percent she does fill out are, in her judgment, necessary to getting her job done. She believes she is successful in part because she knows the difference between what is and isn't superfluous to her function.

Another asks his secretary to call him out of almost every meeting at its midpoint. (He returns to those meetings that he feels are worth his time.) A third brings an egg timer when she chairs task-force and committee sessions. She said about this practice (which of course at first brought smirks to the faces of her peers):

> My mind and spirit get asphyxiated by the repetition, the incredible sterility, of those sessions. On the other hand, if one or two of us

insist on moving things along, if we stubbornly refuse to have our time and minds strangled by the sheer stupidity and the redundancy of hearing the same points endlessly repeated and debated, our meetings become lively, stimulating exchanges, productive beyond all initial expectations.*

Creative adaptors share an ability to listen inwardly and heed the goings-on within. In his lovely early book *The Ultimate Athlete,* George Leonard writes that primitive dance can be viewed as a metaphor for life itself. In tribal dances, we find celebration and sacrament and evidence of the essential dance of life. These dances express primary, fundamental truths about human existence:

It is all a matter of awareness. The more deeply we see into life, the more clearly we perceive the dance. Pursuing reality down into the heart of the atom, we find nothing at all except vibration, music, dancing. And the world of our sense is also dancing. (Leonard, 1975, p. 237)

At their best, within and without, creative adaptors hear this music. Intuitively, they dance.

---

*For an extensive, invaluable list of such activities, see Tom Peter's *Passion for Excellence* (and in particular his chapters on limiting bureaucratic red tape).

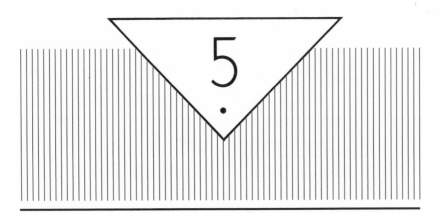

A 21st-CENTURY MIND IS "UNFREAKABLE" AND CHALLENGED BY PROBLEMS

Unfreakability refers not to [our] propensity for burying [our] head in the sand at the sight of danger, but to see the true nature of what is happening and to be able to respond appropriately. This requires a mind which is clear because it is calm.

TIMOTHY GALLWEY, *Inner Game of Tennis*

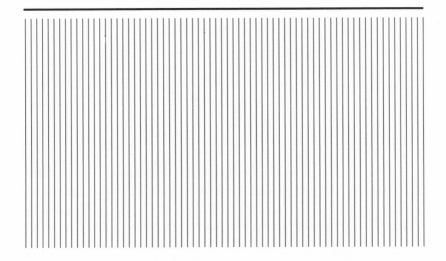

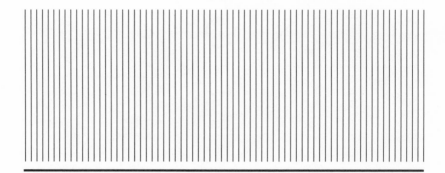

A few years ago the media and medical literature proposed that major life changes could beget illness. Events such as the death of a spouse, a serious illness, a divorce, a move to a new job or community, were found to undermine the average person's physical health, if not his or her comfort and peace of mind. It is certainly understandable that during sudden change or times when we feel we lack control of ourselves or of our futures—as in the case of loss, keen disappointments or illness—we easily become sad, depressed, angry or frightened.

One employee approached me in anguish when her company was suddenly acquired. Her remarks illustrate how rapid, unexpected change can destroy personal stability.

I feel strong emotions welling up, but don't know why. It's sad to see our department breaking up. I experience mood swings. I'm excited at times, and then, close on the heels of that, fearful. The worst part is I feel out-of-control. I imagine that I "should" feel different, and that makes everything worse.

Another person, concerned about his wife after their family's third relocation in ten years, told me these frequent changes had jeopardized their marriage and resulted in his wife's unhappiness:

We expected to build close ties, stable friendships complete with neighborly talks over a back fence about kids, daily life, our ups and downs. We'd hoped our kids would attend one school, not several. Instead, we are transients. Our separations make it too painful to form lifetime friends; we keep our distance from people.

My wife suffers. I'm away all day, busy at the office. I feel connected to people through my business ties. But she's at home, alone. She's grieved for a few years, but won't talk to me about it. She's down in the dumps, and I'm worried.

These comments reveal the predictable cycle of shock and psychological disorientation, the fear, anxiety and mood swings that almost everyone experiences when readjusting to major life-changes. Almost everyone.

For creative adaptors, control over *events* may not be crucial to happiness. Since autonomous, emotionally healthy people tend toward personal integration—a state in which one's feelings, values and diverse inner states are merged so that psychic balance is reached—adjustment to the world is ongoing and constant, not fixed. This internal pliability means that those with a 21st-century mind understand and accept life's impermanence.

One woman said that although initially she disliked the disorder that change introduced after many moves she enjoyed organizing chaos. She felt most stimulated during those times when she had least control over circumstances. "Instead of too stringently protecting myself against life's demands, my self-control during unexpected change has improved. This is key. I try to master myself when facing the unknown, even enjoy the so-called anarchy—this seems my special challenge: The less certainty I need, the more truly secure I know I am."

There seem to be at least three basic reasons why creative adaptives enjoy pitting themselves against odds or obstacles:

- they are flexible when facing change;
- they are unfreakable (to employ Gallwey's term);
- they enjoy the climb up the mountains that change or problems present.

FLEXIBLE AND GROWTH-SEEKING

Much as some individuals crave stability and sameness, others long for change. Creative adaptors may, in fact, seek out life moves that demand their growth as persons. As an extreme example, one man said that relocating to a different state was helpful when he felt a need to express a different side of himself. His personal development was combined with physical rearrangement.

My move helped me shed my old skin precisely because I didn't have to pretend to be my outmoded self. Moving away let me avoid tired conversations with family or friends. In the new place, I don't have to live up to old expectations, am free to explore my options in an entirely fresh way. Traveling used to help me achieve this, but moving to another state is a surer way to develop as an adult.

Other people say job changes or the cultivation of wider circles of friends helps them tap their depths. Creative adaptors often exploit temporary crises or setbacks to set in motion long-term changes about which they may once have only dreamed. For instance, a reader wrote me about a business she wanted to start, and said it was her "1,000th" idea. A personal dislocation, the loss of a job, made her able to act now on the thousandth idea, although she had been pondering the matter for years.

In short, improvisors enjoy and move spontaneously toward flexible experimentation rather than avoid or fear it. They have an appetite for the flavor that personal exploration can add to life. Alvin Toffler's notion of "immobiles" and "modular" persons (Toffler, 1970) helps explain why some people have better improvisational skills than others.

Toffler's immobiles are not simply Third World villagers who spend their whole life in backward hamlets, protected securely by the permanence of family, value or community systems. Rather, an immobile can be *anyone* whose helplessness, negative emotions or idealized images of past glories surfaces when he or she is required to change. For example, individuals who agonize over role, job or interpersonal shifts, or who are entrenched in a single way of being, thinking or behaving, often are unable to break free of outmoded behaviors and emotional sets. They also find it hard to graduate into untried, exploratory responses when life suggests they try something novel. When we lose our job, marriage or health, this may be the very time to grow. Unlike, say, a widower who transmutes a housekeeping hobby into a potentially lucrative bed-and-breakfast after losing a nine-to-five job, immobiles block themselves from finding creative expression and options. They are fixed in a unidimensional world, no matter what the personal cost.

In varying degrees, they suppress and repress their own richness by holding themselves in one rigid frame of reference.

By contrast, flexible persons more easily break old ties, living styles or thinking patterns. This is not to say they are unfeeling, but that they possess greater emotional freedom to choose whatever routines are most appropriate to here-and-now realities. Such people gain stimulation, if not also subjective and economic advantage, by reinterpreting long-standing habits. People who start to travel after retiring, even though they'd been firmly planted in one home or community before that, illustrate this emotional freedom. They are also less psychologically fettered and can choose the untried path because they are not biased against it or subjectively walled off from it. In other words, the individual is willing to give travel—or any other novel behavior—a chance before deciding against it.

The creative person thinks in nonstereotypical, unconventional ways, insightfully spotting his best answers and options, breaking out of intellectual and emotional ruts. As the last chapter shows, the special openness or receptivity of 21st-century thinking results in extremely sensitive antennae; the individual is psychically open, will use anything as a tool to better understand problems or the world at large. To develop this receptivity one must relinquish old thought-modes.

This psychological letting go seems the critical advantage that permits flexibility, creative adaptation and resourceful adjustment to new circumstances. The flexible person carries less emotional baggage into new situations and is also intellectually freer than most others. While not *un*committed to certain sacrosanct variables such as home, former value systems, family or friends, those who relocate, change jobs or make other transitions easily are not unthinkingly committed to sentimental social factors such as their traditional communities or culturally prescribed holidays. As with the man who said relocation helped him shed his "old skin," their moves represent more than just physical dislocations and seem to stimulate inner growth, offering a chance for self-mastery.

The transitory nature of contemporary relationships (to jobs, acquaintances, family, community and institutional systems) indicates that today many of us routinely reinvest ourselves. Most seem eager to develop new skills for personal reinvention. One also wonders if intense, rapid personal evolution is not in itself a primary cause for what seems to be our collective global restlessness. Might not those with creative adaptive skills already have learned something valuable that the rest of humanity can be taught? Viewed in this way, perhaps the need for individual growth prompts external changes, instead of externals always stimulating and driving inner change. As one woman put it, "It seems like my personal growth forced me to revise my life—I've made new friends, changed work and look like a wholly new person, all because on the inside I'm different."

Whatever their future role or current reason for being, people with creative adaptive aptitudes are still in the minority, do not yet represent the bulk of our population. One client admitted, "My appetite for adventure and change makes me a black sheep in my family. I'm completely at a loss to find anyone to talk to about my life. My friends also seem to resent my love of life and my intense involvement with things that interest me. When I have no soap-opera problem to add to our conversations, their disappointment is nearly palpable." To the "normal" person, it still may be natural to suppress spontaneity and distinctiveness as a way to fit in or adjust. For creative adaptives, such normality will feel like an unhealthy defense, an unnatural straitjacket that thwarts the impulses and primary instincts of a full, rich life.

ENJOYING THE CLIMB

In her inspiring autobiographical comments on the joys and hardships of solo canoeing, author Audrey Sutherland describes one reason she returns to unforgiving, treacherous waters:

> I had to go back again. To be that terrified of anything, that incompetent, survive by that small a margin—I'd better analyze, practice, then return and do it right. (Sutherland, 1986, p. 85)

Although Sutherland writes that the special beauty of the wilderness and waters—not challenges—motivate her return, she also admits that fear is more a barrier than the problem feared. She finds it unacceptable to give in to fear or to the need for comfort and safety. Whatever their goals, many creative, achieving adults thrive on overcoming. They enjoy the stimulation of being challenged by the unknown. Over and over again we see that such people put themselves into circumstances where their courage, tenacity and ingenuity can be tested, exercised and then extended.

The more creative we are, the more possible it is we will invent personal problems if our minds lack complex challenges. Awareness is usually all that's needed to circumvent this occurrence. Just knowing that our minds need to be used, as our bodies' muscles need using, is generally sufficient. The upshot of "climbing new mountains" is this: We feel ourselves growing competent and we sense ourselves increasing in inner wealth as we master hardship or grow in thinking skills. The self-inventive or reinventive process, postponement of gratification, the exercise of courage, tenacity and leaps into the unknown—these movements, although arduous and temporarily stress-increasing, are somehow strangely necessary to the creative adaptor's feeling of self-fulfillment. More than most, the creative adaptive sacrifices short-term comfort for long-term gain.

It is essential to grasp the ability factors at play here. The psychoanalyst Karen Horney once distinguished neurotic from healthy striving. She wrote that all neurotic striving emanates from weakness, but that healthy people reach out to be, do and have more from the wellsprings of their strength. In keeping with her observations, I suggest that creative adaptives aspire to mastery and to meaningful, dynamic self-expression because of their development. For instance, they are able to discipline themselves for the highly valued, long-term goals or futures their minds envision. One person may express this by seeking outdoor adventure, another through art or invention, yet a third by making some special sacrificial contribution to family, community or vocation. The critical standard or measurement is not simply the result or performance but the person's ability. Strength, talent and psychic maturity calls them into untried regions of effort much as children are called to play. One fast-track young executive said, "I love hard work and the feel of myself under the gun, being fully tested. I have skill and need to use it!" As we consider ourselves, or those who repeatedly attempt to conquer personally relevant objectives, we must not overlook the obvious: Some people are psychologically and intellectually capable of efforts that seem, to others, impossible or even unattractive.*

---

*Many people automatically assume themselves (or others) to be "workaholics" just because passion, energy and tireless effort is expended on behalf of vocational pursuits. However, there is enormous difference between "workaholism" and genius or vocational integration. If we jump to simplistic conclusions, we do the topic a disservice. (For a lengthy discussion on this issue, see Chapter 9 of my book *Do What You Love, the Money Will Follow,* or John Gardner's inspiring short volume *No Easy Victories.* About the fun in hard work, Gardner writes, "Recreational games are . . . the least exciting games . . . [The most exciting games] involve more fully the intellectual resources and the values and social motivations of [humans]—science, teaching, government . . .

A client, and now good friend, epitomizes this profile. The man, whom I'll call "M," heads an international research and development division of a huge multinational corporation. We met during his first day on the job as his division's senior vice president. It was also my first day there, as a human resource adviser to the division's top-management team. After greeting each another and settling into some easy small talk, I casually said we all had a tremendous amount of work ahead of us. Before my remark, M had been serious and standoffish, but at my comment he broke out in a wide grin, answering, "Yeah. And we'll go home every day exhausted, completely worn out. . . . Won't it be fun?!"

M's enthusiasm for a tough assignment, the pleasure he gets out of giving all-out effort to that which he defines as meaningful and his ability to delay short-term gratification for a long-term vision are all emblematic of someone who strives from strength, not from weakness or neuroticism. This brings up another point. I once heard someone say that although everyone says they want to get to the top of the mountain, what most people really want is just to sit around at the mountain's base, sipping hot chocolate and keeping warm. While they may enjoy gazing up at its peak or get "high" by daydreaming about arriving at its summit, many people really fear the dangers or pain of the climb and lack the psychic staying power that achievement demands.

Creative adaptors are problem seekers. They enjoy the arduous work and upward-trek of problem solving. They love using their brains. Moreover, as noted, they are usually psychologically capable of facing and solving complex, long-term puzzles. Viewing problems as challenges, these individuals normally refuse to do the same task again and again. Like one man who told me he leaves a job when he stops learning, creative adaptors may prefer not-knowing to states of certainty or guarantees. Not-knowing stimulates and excites their sense of adventure. This does not mean such people are constantly chasing the unknown, change or risk, but that they have greater options to choose whatever they want. On hearing my remark about sitting at the base of the mountain versus climbing it, a friend put it this way:

For me, "not-knowing" means I'm free to take whatever path seems best on a moment's notice—even the path of "sipping hot chocolate" at times if that's what's right for me.

companionship, novelty, risk, chance-taking, skill, team play, competition and all the other attributes of diversion. And they mean something.") (P. 32)

Her comment helps us see the relatively high self-esteem such a posture requires. The more secure one feels, the greater and more complete any exploration becomes, but the less compulsively one does anything.

It sometimes follows that someone who has been everywhere and done everything renounces material striving and turns inward, for the spiritual quest knows no boundaries and can be traveled for a lifetime. This was the case of a woman I interviewed who had achieved tremendous business success early in her career. Another, a former physician, exhibited the need for "the climb": He became a writer of fiction. His comment, "Writing is the first thing I've ever done that has no achievement ceiling—no matter how expert I become, there is always more to learn," demonstrates that adventure or learning is lifelong.

Robert Schwartz, head of Tarrytown Conference Center, a meeting place where businesspersons learn about our era's trends, once described his old friend Margaret Mead as an "entrepreneur," saying Mead raised common sense to a new level. This contribution or trait seems shared by all creative adaptors, not just business-world innovators. Their projects, transitions or personal achievement, their life's results, make others reflect on what they have done. We wonder how it would feel to do this ourselves. Their achievements inspire and motivate us, and they trigger new mental models and ideals for what is possible.

I do not, of course, advocate change or the dissolution of traditions and long-standing ties simply for change's sake. Nor do I hold up creative adaptors as folk heroes for our age as the arbiters of rapid change. For one thing, emotionally mature, creative adaptive persons with well-defined entrepreneurial skills also enjoy sameness. Most are quite willing and content to work through their boredom, and over the years they become more, rather than less, faithful to tradition, family, or profession. Ritualistic routines or solitary disciplines, such as classical meditation, long-distance running or other physical or philosophical disciplines, seem a fitting alternative to self-imposed job changes, relocations or to initiating endless strings of businesses. I have heard people say that meditation or daily jogging affords them tremendous coping and stress-management advantages. Running, as one example, cultivates endurance and extends people's strength for almost all commitments. They become focused and concentrated while at work, compete against their own previous achievements and sustain enthusiasm for their existing life, family and work. For those who adopt personal disciplines, despite having maintained their commitments for many decades, their loyalty increases rather than decreases over time.

Both commitment to change and the love of routine seem to be two of many ways of creatively answering the question of how to stay an otherwise tedious course over the lengthy haul of a lifetime. Such practices simultaneously build creative adaptive skill and give us the ability to spot or invent options. We are free to choose how we will stay our life's course because we have the self-mastery to choose our best route—not one we fear is externally prescribed or forced upon us, and nothing that we are slavishly addicted to pursue.

UNFREAKABLE

Although Gallwey's term "unfreakability" refers to the emotional detachment required for an effective tennis game or cool business negotiation, the notion has wider utility. This focus and single-mindedness, this nonattached stance, can be the underpinning for our whole life when it is our dominant way of being—not simply a technique. Unfreakability means being centered, retaining inner balance and a kind of emotional clarity or unshakable faith in a productive outcome. This fuels right actions, especially when we face multiple options. Anyone who has ever lost a job because of a company closing or a merger knows how important it is to keep calm and to think of one's best alternatives. Those whose negative imaginations or feelings take over are much less likely to smoothly make a transition during times of crisis or personal pressure.

Creative adaptors often yearn to work exclusively on projects or goals that have had meaning since early childhood or adolescence. Rather than squander valuable time or energy thinking about the past or what others are doing or having anxious feelings about an uncertain future, they demonstrate an uncanny ability to bring their predominant life's vision into being. Our next chapter suggests that each creative adaptive person embodies a unique dialectic that is apparent in his or her problems and preferred solutions. For now, it helps to realize that unfreakability is aided when we have purpose and direction.

A young woman who read my book on right livelihood resonated with the idea that personal vision can infuse someone's entire life with energy and healthful drive.

I am nineteen years old. I have never been content with society's day-to-day grinds. And, although I was raised by abusive, superficial parents, I have always valued humanity, the earth, and all of life.

I left high school a year early because there was literally nothing there for me. I had almost nothing in common with my peers. [They] were involved with fair-weather fads and rock groups; I was fascinated by politics, pollution and endangered species. I also knew these to be good interests—proof of this is how well I have done in college so far.

The thing I wanted to tell you is that I have started an ecology-centered business out of my home. And, just a few months ago, I started publishing my poetry and essays along with other people's work, as another offshoot of the first organization. My husband supports me wholeheartedly and we work together. . . . He works full time, while I [study], run these businesses and do the housework.

This woman's life directions clearly presented themselves to her at an early age. Many others, if not all who fit the psychological description under discussion, have said the identical thing: Their talents, values or goals "called" them in some coherent, consistent yet novel way. For those answering this call, their ordinary day-to-day choices flow, as do their crisis choices. They are stamped with the imprint or logo of their own distinctiveness. The choices represent the person, rather than being merely a collection of haphazard, random acts reflecting parents, peers, dominant cultural trends or values of the time.

During times of increased pressure or change, single-mindedness also stabilizes life. It adds to our unshakable faith in what we are trying to accomplish. Even though at the moment of choice-making we may feel highly charged, fragmented, emotional or reactive, over the long haul of our lifetime, if we have been focused, our general "tone" and direction of life seem all of a piece, unified, coherent.

One young man in his twenties told me that when he changed his major in college from science to liberal arts, his parents, especially his father, became so upset that a special family meeting was called to dissuade him. He had been expected to follow the family's academic tradition of math and science. All his respected relatives were scientists. It was unthinkable for him to consider anything else, especially his new intended areas of study, marketing or teaching. Today, as a liberal arts graduate, he advises senior management of small firms how to gain marketplace dominance in their field. His business success is rooted in his early commitment to do what he sensed was his right livelihood. He has been able to weather the economic storms of entrepreneuring because he is inwardly centered.

Another person confided that he had always wanted to be a poet but entered a "respectable profession" in order to be financially successful. Now, twenty-five years later, he feels that if he doesn't change his career, he will have wasted his life. Although he put his early sense of what he needed on hold, his desire waited patiently, much as a loyal friend or lover waits for us for years while we are busy with something else. When we are ready, they are still there. In this same way, we can often retrieve early life plans.

Purposefulness also begets endurance. An artist I'll call "SW" says her tenacity during a grave illness taught her she could trust herself to plod on, despite an all-time low in physical and psychic energy. She continued to work at her craft, building her reputation as an artist because she was so clear that her intentions were central to her life's joy. Today her artwork is healthier than ever. So is she. She learned that her efforts were sustainable because she brought an intense drive to her vision:

Even at age four, I had enormous drive. I knew I wanted to be an artist. This has always been my need. I have given up food to buy art materials, and I have always had this tendency. I recall telling another artist friend that if I had only money enough to buy a head of lettuce or a piece of wood to make a frame, I'd buy the wood. He couldn't understand that. But it is clear to me that the difference between someone with this energy and someone without it is the ability to endure and ultimately succeed, if only in a personal sense.

Choice-making such as this flows. This fluidity also makes comprehensible that which is not. Lofty, clear purpose lifts us out of the unintelligible, emotional confusion of ordinary existence (what Buber calls "the commotion of human life") and lets us touch high feelings and our most refined, intuitive reflexes. One individual described his emotional nonattachment from the perspective of his practice of martial arts, in particular linking it to what is called Nirvana—the intense clarity and beauty of the world as it is perceived during spiritual enlightenment:

Perhaps the best example of flow comes from the martial arts in general and [for me, kung fu and t'ai chi in particular. As a student of these arts] I immediately identified with your notion of flow. The feeling that emerges during the correct performance of a technique or form is an odd sort of objectivity.

Students are encouraged to see nothing, but to focus their perception on using energy (chi) to control their bodies with maximum precision. This turning of the intellect to tasks usually delegated to the subconscious mind creates, first, an isolation of purpose that transcends [the body and externals].

Second, an abstract, unbiased view of the circumstances surrounding the body is gained. Finally, a sort of bliss that makes everything appear to happen in slow motion as the mind-body unit evaluates and reacts surely to its environment.

As I mentioned earlier, selected martial arts are often apt metaphors for creative adaptation's qualities. Practiced rightly, these arts enhance our spontaneous and instant responses to outer circumstances. This person's remarks also provide an excellent outline of the way in which advanced Positive Structuring works. By practicing almost any martial arts noncompetitively, we train ourselves to be physically poised for whatever comes along. We also learn to be self-possessed, to stay cool and unfreakable under "real life" pressures, deadlines or change. Our instinctive responses will grow to be appropriate for the demands of any moment—not just in the practice of our discipline. With respect to training ourselves to be flexible yet committed, martial arts seem to be ideal models for structuring the poised, balanced yet active life-stance we may want.

The relaxed alertness called for by almost all martial arts (especially the nonattack varieties) demonstrates high creative adaptive skill on a physical plane. I frequently suggest that clients study aikido or judo, especially when they are easily angered, frazzled or overreactive. I have come to believe that psychologists and psychiatrists can better help people improve their lives by introducing them to a full "mix" of transformational agents. Art, sport, dance, deep tissue massage, and selected physical disciplines seem excellent adjuncts to the mental health "sciences." Since emotional objectivity is essential for gaining life-mastery, martial arts, meditation and numerous other noncompetitive disciplines can help us if used wisely.

Flow of choices and objectivity are not attributes limited to kung-fu experts, artists or poets. Rather, all who identify and are moved by a hum of inner direction can eventually achieve these qualities. Just how we arrive at such inner direction is still a question, largely a mystery. Some people quite obviously gain it early in childhood, while others search their whole lives for what they sense they must be or do. A seventy-year-old man told me he had wasted his life because he hadn't found his true vocation. The haunting feeling that something is missing accompanies some people all their life, and their deepest purpose eludes them no matter how they search. On the other hand, more often than we imagine, people simply create their vocations, life-purposes and meanings. Then they jump into these with gusto and a spirit of high adventure. If they translate their personal truths, vision or values successfully, there is not much in the world that can throw them off balance.

POSITIVE STRUCTURING: "CONSTRUCTING" YOUR OWN INNER CALM

To cultivate an inner calm that endures even during chaos, we need to design a long-term, multistep Positive Structuring program, to construct our habit of calm over time, so that the trait takes root. Our first phase always describes "what," while Phase II delves deeply into the nuances of the thing. Generally, as we come to understand this technique, the second phase just naturally evolves out of the first. Initially, we ask ourselves what inward stability feels like. Questions like "What makes me experience myself as calm?," "When have I felt balanced and harmonious?," "What thoughts bring me peace of mind?" help us. We may spend a few days (or longer) specifically developing a precise language that outlines the essence of this characteristic. We try to describe the elements of what we want as we know them. This first step permits entry into the world of inner calm, shows us its spirit.*

Next, we begin to establish ourselves in this world to live in it and adopt its spirit. We usually can find a piece of beautifully written music or prose that opens us to the heart of the matter. For example, Robert Grundin's *Time and the Art of Living* contains many such passages. One is about people who are "complete in the present." Attentive, alert and self-possessed, such people make Grundin feel ". . . that their lives

---

*See Anthony Robbins's book *Unlimited Power*, for helpful exercises for producing what in the language of neurolinguistic programming are called states.

possess a kind of qualified eternity; that past and future, birth and death, meet for them as in the completion of a circle." (Grundin, 1982, p. 209) Or, we can recall times and activities that were calming. Our remembrances are unique to the context of our life, and seem the best way of bringing us into the universe of our goals. When I was a child, my mother and grandmother insisted I stop playing each afternoon and join them for tea. Teatime was at four o'clock every day. For me this was a soothing, pretty time, a civilizing constant when many other facets of life were crumbling. There was an established protocol for every detail of this ritual. Before tea, hands were washed and hair was combed. During tea, there was a proper way to pour, stir or drink tea. I was instructed how to sit, talk and request my leave. Our prearranged appointment helped compose my day; this single habit structured life and, consequently, emotions. Gradually, teatime at the very least imprinted the possibility of sanity and order on my mind. Years later, when reading about the Japanese tea ceremony, I understood why this simple tradition was elevated into an elegant art form.

In my own book on choices (1988), I describe how daily choices affect our psyches, self-esteem and our awareness. Similarly, Alexandra Stoddard's lovely book *Living a Beautiful Life* is full of uncomplicated, soothing daily rituals that can be adopted to enhance inner calm. Stoddard defines "ritual" as those daily patterns and small embellishments that improve the way we do ordinary things. Since her professional background is interior design, she approaches choice-making from a ceremonial and environmental perspective. However we prefer to come at this, if we can create one or two rituals by which to grow centered, then Phase III's study models quite easily fall into place. Our rituals become our models and vice versa.

If I were designing a physical study model for myself, I might reenact a daily teatime, even if it was only an improved, more conscious way of taking a coffee break at work. Or, I might meditate in a busy place—the ladies' lounge of the O'Hare Airport, for example—or seek out the one or two most negative persons I knew, invite them to lunch and then practice maintaining my positive outlook and poise. On the other hand, I could invite positive types and use the lunch as a time for observation and learning. There are endless options. All this is done quietly, as innocent, childlike exploration. We simply develop harmless, private projects by which we teach ourselves about the world of selected traits or behaviors and in so doing learn about ourselves. Our practice is steady and low-key—not in any way ambitious or aggressive.

As much as possible we incorporate our projects into our usual routines. Many other physical or experiential models can culture tranquillity. For instance, consider the following:

- *Control of insignificant acts.* Gandhi wrote that no matter how unimportant the thing we have to do, we make huge strides in our personal development if we pay as much attention to the small act as to the large. I find attentive, mindful acts to be centering as well.
- *Reading poetry or scriptures.* Instead of tea or coffee breaks, we can read bits of high, sacred writings to inspire, bring us to our best self and to calm or soothe us. Many people say that a ten-minute reading break, during the day or right after lunch, alters their outlook for the better, slows down and deepens their breathing rate (as in meditation), strengthens motivation and lifts moral tone.
- *Boatbuilding.* Although I have never tried it, I imagine that building anything, but especially a boat, car, plane or other handcrafted vehicle, is enormously stress-reducing. Building a ship in a bottle—perhaps in lieu of a heavy lunch—is another self-centering device to structure inner calm.

In the sixties and seventies, Gestalt therapists used to assign psychological tasks to their clients. "Put your anger in a chair," they would say. "Tell your anger what you feel right now." We can put inner peace, prosperity or creative adaptation, "in a chair," can listen to ourselves as we have dialogue with these elements. Or we can write about these in a journal. What do we want from these qualities? Why have they eluded us thus far? What is our "payoff" for living in high commotion? What would we have to do, what would we give up, if we were to adopt a nondoing, passive, goal*less* spirit? If we turn in, toward ourselves, listening steadily in a meditative way, with wonder and trust, soon, without strong emotion, we fuse with our goal, "know it" in a unitive way that affords us meta-insight.

In some unfathomable way, once we come into the deepest level of our own interior calm, we "know" only profound silence. Such silence has always existed in us, always will exist. It undergirds our life. This silence or level of awareness is the subtlest silent music of our own consciousness, the sound of one hand clapping.

Lest we think this sequence too complex, be assured that even children can—and do—understand how to reach their own deep silence and structure inner calm into their way of being. A friend's seven-year-old son is learning t'ai chi at his school. The father of one of the other children—a t'ai chi master—volunteers his time weekly to teach the children how to practice this art of movement. Last week this child showed his parents what he had learned from his practice that day: how to sit perfectly still for three minutes. (I know sixty-five-year-olds who cannot manage this.) Later, through repetition, this seven-year-old invented his own slow, graceful movements, naming them to his liking. He is using an interactive, representational exercise to extend himself as a person into untried arenas of skill. This is Positive Structuring. It's so simple, a child can do it. Perhaps that's why we adults have so much trouble—it's too simple.

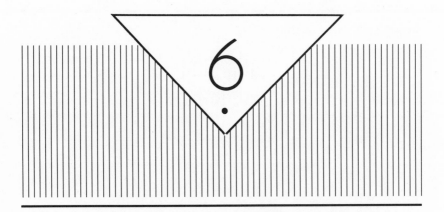

A 21st-CENTURY MIND
ENJOYS ORDERING
CHAOS

All of your anxiety is because of your desire
for harmony. Seek disharmony; then you
will gain peace.

RUMI

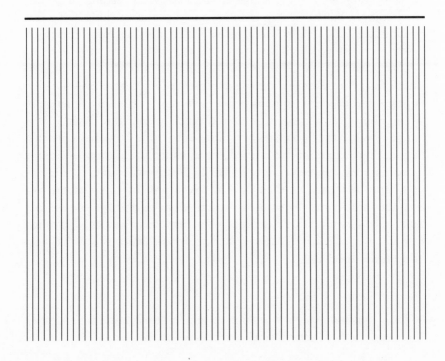

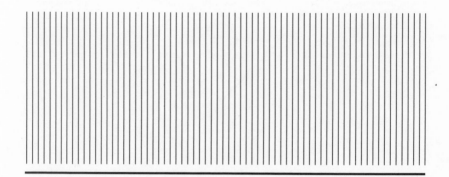

A 21st-century mind and what ancients call "enlightenment" seem closely related. As our awareness is increasingly influenced by unitive consciousness, we develop wholeness. Our perception changes, answers flow; we are enhanced personally, gaining what the Buddhists call a big mind, an open mind.

This movement makes us increasingly optimistic and effective. We handle discontinuities in an improved, coherent fashion—even in a playful way. It is this big mind that eventually lets us remain calm and centered in the midst of disharmony. Now we more easily sort priorities when, previously, we felt overwhelmed or out of control or lacked concentration for routine activities such as work, reading or simple conversation. When, as its norm, our mind begins to think along discontinuous lines, we become receptive to nonconscious messages, fleeting insight and hunches.

Ideally, each of us can learn to be comfortable in a transient existence, since life *is* flux. But few people automatically accept changes easily. A priest and friend of mine says he knows he "should take change in stride," but after a certain point too much wears him down. "It is fatiguing when the floodgates of options open up and too many alternatives appear. Then I get confused and anxious." While the desire for harmony seems universal, it is primarily creative adaptives who interpret times of chaos as their call to adventure. In this chapter, we examine how such persons approach work-related problems, but should keep in mind that any type of disorder can be managed in much the same way. Creative adaptives share several characteristics that help bring order to chaos:

- Their dynamic insight is stabilizing and lets their minds move easily beyond current knowledge into fresh solutions.

- They are fully absorbed in their personal quest for answers.
- Their unique thinking process may be known to them and reveals a personal dialectic, or unfolding. They solve larger life-questions when tackling smaller, situational ones.

DYNAMIC INSIGHT PROVIDES INNER STABILITY

Dr. A. Reza Arasteh, whose transcultural study of enlightened individuals, *Final Integration in the Adult Personality*, helped my understanding of this subject, calls persons who can move effortlessly through personal transitions "fully integrated." He outlines their multifaceted complex of virtues, and also reminds us that such individuals' perceptual field is imperturbable, timeless, regionless. In them we do not find culturally narrow behaviors or values, but rather broad-gauged, widely applicable, very human characteristics. In fact, Arasteh's other phrase for fully integrated is *universal self.*＊

For example he describes scholar and theologian Al-Ghazzali (d., A.D. 1111) as one who was familiar with the unitive experience, and who believed that this enormously increased his creative power. His receptive state was far beyond that of ordinary beings. For Arasteh, the fully integrated exist in a continual state of dynamic insight. Their dynamism, more than almost any other factor, enables them to take whatever comes in stride, promotes grace-under-pressure. I believe dynamic insight to be simply a normal function of any highly developed mind. This trait might seem extraordinary to those of us who struggle to keep everything in our lives under control and within neat and tidy boundaries, but is—to repeat the Buddhist phrase—nothing special. Dynamic insight, true interior quiet or deep imperturbability is a potential that each of us is meant to experience. This mind easily moves beyond itself, finds a silent home of calm within itself and hears its own intuitive intelligence, regardless of what else is going on. This mind's blend of assets makes quick sense of nonsense.

We rarely cultivate such dynamic insight in a single effort or pristine burst. Rather, this occurs incrementally, over the course of a life whose sole purpose is to practice unfolding its own potential in creatively intelligent action. Many, if not most, still resist the challenge of ultimate

---

＊Arasteh's comparisons of Goethe, Rumi and other universal thinkers is well worth a review.

mental health and full potential. While it is beyond the scope of this book to explore the reason for our normal resistance to growth or health, we do postpone our good. This challenge for complete development is the deepest, most radical call of our human existence. Almost everyone fears—and craves—this call. Jung called it finding our true vocation. He wrote often of the mixed blessings this pursuit entailed, said it is at once a "charism and a curse," involving us in ongoing work of transmutation. During this long process, while we are growing conscious, we must pull away from group and personal unconsciousness. Jung cautioned us to be ready for an isolated time—a lonely experience. There was, he wrote, no other, more reassuring way to describe it. (Jung, 1954)

Largely because of our need for love and belonging and our fear of isolation, we avoid our deepest truths or virtues and shy away from our own unfolding. Or, we attempt to master ourselves and our circumstances in harsh ways that destroy us and damage others. Initially, we face predictable conflicts when "trying" too hard to grow or control unknowns.

MOVING BEYOND THE KNOWN IS PLEASURABLE

During our struggle to achieve meaningful answers or goals, we can move beyond what we know for clues about what's needed only if we let go of what's familiar. The unknown either terrifies or unsettles us or it can be fascinating—a stimulating playground where we meet our own dynamic insight. I've heard people say that the disorder of an uncharted assignment or project helped them realize how independent and capable they were. Although initially they were frightened to leave familiar territory, later their minds structured something useful in a way that added new texture or richness to their entire lives. They express a side of themselves they'd only dreamed about. Had such individuals been unable to tolerate the confusion of a temporary vacuum—for instance, a loss of a relationship, job or certain sacrosanct ideas—they would not have met their human powers.

I'm reminded of a man appointed to head up his corporation's Asian division. After the hoopla of his promotion, he discovered he *was* the division—a unit of one. Knowing no one in Asia, he and his family transferred overseas. He alone set up an office, hired a secretary, leased office equipment and furniture while his wife managed the foreign home front. Finally, logistics handled, he realized no one else was around to instruct him about what to do next. "I panicked. There were no monthly meetings about goals and objectives. I didn't speak the language. I had no manager to pat me on the back or get me going and no professional contacts. It was a big void—I'd never set my own priorities in exactly this way before." One step at a time, he structured an otherwise too open-ended situation. In a few months, he began to feel that this was the most fun he'd ever had. Soon he doubted that he could ever work "for" anyone again. He found his dynamic insight, and this made him appreciate, and enjoy, his creative adaptive power. If we hope to uncover our own best thinking patterns, it helps to notice what we do when placed in similarly unstructured situations or when faced with problems we don't automatically know how to solve.

An attorney described his own vague, creative movement as pleasurable and quite rudimentary—as very ordinary:

I enjoy uncertainty in my daily work. No two days are ever the same. No two cases are ever alike, if only that the people I meet are completely different. I continually expand my skill as a lawyer and my knowledge of the law. But also I learn about myself as I'm putting crooked things straight in my mind. This this sorting out teaches me so much.

Probably because thinking is so basic a drive for me, I get gut pleasure out of handling complex cases that no one else wants to tackle. The harder, more impossible the case, the better I like it—but not to show off or prove myself. I just enjoy working with, getting to know, my intrinsic wisdom, hunches, my own inner impulses.

Not everyone enjoys impossible-to-solve problems. No two people are exactly alike in this. A biochemical physicist I will call CD admits he thoroughly relishes tough projects, but not when they are hopeless or cannot be brought to closure.

I like problems that I think I can solve. There have been some that I never completed. Although I knew they'd be tough when I began working on them, after beating my head against the wall for a few years, I decided to change directions, stop working on them for a while.

This doesn't mean I've given up thinking about them. However, my thinking goes underground. I keep working the thing under the conscious surface of my awareness: my dreams, informal conversations and hobbies all seem to further my inquiry.

In itself, the upheaval involved in not-knowing is most stimulating when we trust ourselves. Searching out answers, waiting for insights to come from fragments and bits of information that we pull together—in short, "researching" ourselves—involves a predictable detective process as well as a cycle of emotional and intellectual ups and downs. This often long-term process is an important part of ordering chaos. Just as children enjoy roller-coaster rides or love hearing ghost stories while safely huddled around a cozy campfire, so, in our serious hunt for answers, we adults can find entertainment of high order.

The word *research* means to investigate, to track down or follow clues to an endpoint of resolution. CD describes the fun of this chase:

> There is a hunt to the analysis process that I find really fun. Trying to solve things, hopefully in a logical manner, is my delight. I thrill knowing my mind *can* solve it. My adrenaline increases when I find my experimentation design working. Aside from intellectual excitement, I gain extreme fulfillment working on a scientific team that pulls together to accomplish something. In our small lab, pulling together is the norm—and it's rewarding.

Apparently, his enjoyment is obvious—not just to him, but also to his small daughter:

> I usually internalize problems, bring them all the way down into me. I just can't skim the surface. I take my work home with me, stew about chemistry: I even dream about molecules. I can see or visualize the molecules flipping around in reaction.
>
> I must do something outwardly to signal this process is occurring. Perhaps I'm extra-animated. Definitely, I'm enthused. My daughter notices this. She says she likes to see me like this. But I also notice she backs off a bit. That's probably because, without even having been told, she knows I need to incubate ideas, have a bit of space or

privacy to probe and pull together all these little bits of data that I've gathered.

CHAOS AS PLAY

Author, educator, philosopher, scientist Jacob Bronowski reminds us that creative discovery is a natural expression of the human community. In every culture known, no matter how "primitive," some sort of exploration occurs. Classic stories of heroic (or even strikingly mundane) searches for answers unfold like suspenseful mystery novels: Columbus's hunt for what he believed was a new continent; Crick and Watson's work to authenticate the structure of the DNA molecule; a poet's quest for the right word or line for a simple bit of haiku; a man, woman, boy or girl's search for a remedy for their mysterious illness—all these, and similar examples of our own, make for dramatic retelling and reflection. There is high adventure in disorder and in not-knowing, because rummaging for clues and answers is exciting.

When my clients get involved with their study models, their absorption "lifts" them out of worry and self-concern. Involvement activates a healthy mental response: invention, discovery and the creative process. Resourceful, productive thinking stimulates superpsychic impulses and even optimism. Most people report that, especially when engrossed in a manageable problem, their dreams and daytime reflections take on an amusing, puzzle-solving feel that they like.

The artist SW, quoted in Chapter 5, says her characteristic artistic disarray is both enjoyable and terrifying. Her comments reveal the close link between excitement when facing the unknown and apprehension:

> Chaos is a part of my artistic process. I never repeat myself in a painting if I've done one I consider "successful." This is also true of my teaching: I do not teach typical art courses—I don't want to parrot myself. Repeating myself is too hard, even though creating a fresh, untried approach takes more time and energy.
>
> I approach my job [as administrator of an artists' collective] with the same process: At first, the depth of a problem seems scary (like when I was negotiating for our new building). I don't know exactly what to do. I live on trust and experimentation. And, I wait—I wait

to figure it out, or learn, what to do. I wait for inner clarification. This always comes about. Eventually, I am able to see how to sort things out and solve problems to my satisfaction. This is my predictable cycle.

SW's "waiting" illustrates what passive, trust-filled, nondoing is like in a healthy creative achiever. Learning about, then accommodating, our own creative process—despite fear or uncertainty—can change our life for the better. Certainly, we grow in self-confidence and trust as a result. By stretching our ability to be intuitively creative in day-to-day matters, we build self-discipline, which enhances self-esteem. As we observe ourselves honoring our own interests, or style of concentration or most effective work idiosyncrasies, we also notice ourselves strengthening other competencies naturally, without making a conscious effort to "work on ourselves." Progressively difficult challenges may seem manageable and in time even become exciting. Or we may notice ourselves able to stay with a task longer, have more physical or intellectual endurance.

POSITIVE STRUCTURING FOR ORDERING CAREER UNCERTAINTIES

As we practice Positive Structuring, our own creative process turns into intelligent, organizing action. This is certainly true when the method is applied to career unknowns. A client I'll call "Ben" sought satisfying employment but felt assaulted by the many changes in his profession. The corporation in which he worked was aggressively acquiring other smaller firms. Ben's department was in a constant state of upheaval. When examining the lot of his colleagues in other national companies, he found them no better off. Ben was financially able to shift careers entirely, but felt overwhelmed by this thought: "This is a big move for me—I'm baffled. I don't know where to start or what issues to examine."

Initially, even before activating Positive Structuring's first phase, Ben simply had to identify his goals. What did he really want to do? What could he productively offer an employer? Seeing the whole world open up to him, Ben knew he had to narrow his focus and decide what piece of this expanse was for him. This meant he needed to ask himself some grounding questions:

- What are my natural talents?
- How and when do I gain my best insights?
- What is my memory, or history, of personal successes and fulfillments?
- When do I feel particularly motivated or fulfilled?
- What do I require to improve or revise my initial insights or to bring projects to completion?
- What kind of work space and corporate culture do I prefer?
- How much privacy and silence do I need?
- Do I work best alone or with others, in a team?
- What type of people do I prefer to be around?
- What kind of idiosyncratic habits or feedback further, or diminish, my efforts?
- When do I withdraw energy and resist?
- What values, visions or purposes do I hope to express through my life?
- When does my enthusiasm, laziness, daydreaming, physical movements, etc., further my efforts?*

Ben's self-inquiry showed him that he wanted to remain in his profession, but that he would be happiest in an academic environment.

ENTERING THE SPIRIT OF YOUR GOAL

Phase I and II: Exploration—Discovering "What":

Such initial, open-ended and fairly long-term explorations simply produce data. Our first Positive Structuring step is always to *describe* "what"—enter the spirit of a permanence *within ourselves* that we hope to create amid an impermanent world. We do this in as many ways as possible. Answering such broad questions stabilizes us and usually results in newfound confidence. For example, when conducting an exec-

---

*Anyone interested in a book of such organizing questions (and their life-style or value relevance) should read Richard Bolles's classic *What Color Is Your Parachute?* For journal work, one of the best books is Progoff's *Intensive Journal Workshop*.

utive development session with senior managers whose functions have been eliminated due to corporate restructurings or mergers, I generally ask them questions such as those listed above. Our discussion may span one or two sessions. Sometimes I make other, equally general inquiries that people cannot answer immediately and on which they must reflect alone, over time. My purpose is to have people understand that with or without the company there is something that they can do and do well. It is always best if we can instill in ourselves the feeling, "With or without a paid, nine-to-five, structured position, I intend to work at this or that job, task, career, vocation." Sara, a woman I interviewed, learned to inquire of herself, "What would I want to be doing if this restructuring (or illness, job loss, divorce, relocation, etc.) hadn't happened?" Then, with confidence and full faith, we can realize the objective and move toward it. Such questions (and answers) help us know, and accept, who we are. In this way, we begin to work with or accommodate the unknown, fuse our inner and outer realities. We see we have within us what we need to answer complex questions. In time we meet our inner core with a progressively fearless, open mind.

At this point, Ben found it helpful to record his feelings in a journal. He had read a number of books and articles about career changing and wrote down his worries about making the transition as well as his hopes and dreams about what he ideally wanted to contribute professionally. He found inspirational quotes and anecdotes about others who had faced the same problem, and all these notes triggered confidence as well as clarity about his directions. When Ben finally began sending out his résumé, he knew precisely what he wanted.

I still wish I could stay put. But the world's changing, and at least I know that if I want to work in a particular way, I'm going to have to create that opportunity for myself. It won't just happen automatically.

Ideally, we strive to preserve what is real and valuable within ourselves. We separate our core truths from the exigencies and demands of our outer life. Our Phase I investigation is not a quick fix; rather, it brings us into our own light, opens us to our own big mind. Finding our own best method or process of self-inquiry (regardless of the issue) means we ultimately must understand our own problem-solving process. This is a lengthy, meandering procedure. It is introspective and often a trial-and-error affair. A speedy journal list or one set of written goals, while supportive, is rarely enough. In Ben's case, reading books and magazine articles was coupled with notes in a journal. In the area of our own research, the following are useful prompts for gathering the kernels of self-truths amid a field of confusion:

- Photographs that clearly illustrate what we want or stimulate insight.
- Poetry—even a few, well-chosen and meaningful lines that describe what we're hoping to find, say, create or do.
- Music—especially an inspiring or invigorating piece that reminds us of something fine and elevated in ourselves that we want to bring to life through this or that goal.
- Conversation—talking about our quest or problem with a trusted other, like a spiritual director or best friend, can elicit important insights,
- Visualization exercises can help us contact a part of ourselves that is generally hidden from our conscious mind.*

Positive Structuring tasks like these unfold our concerns in an organic, natural progression. Sometimes defining what we want, then entering the spirit of the thing happens simultaneously, flows together. To think that we should devote one, uninterrupted hour to Phase I research and another, separate, uninterrupted session to Phase II is to oversimplify the process. While for some projects and objectives neatly divided sessions work like a charm, others won't follow this exact pattern. If we can allow ourselves time to obey our intuitive sequencing and timing of each phase and project, we will be able to live with our feelings (and solutions) as long as necessary before rushing along to the next. This living with a matter lets us mediate on our aspirations, our flaws or limitations and the truth inherent in our present circumstances in a way that surfaces many important insights or admissions.

In this vein, not everyone (and not every goal) requires an advanced, metaphorical model. Ben moved rapidly from anxious not-knowing to identifying his next career move. Then he simply took concrete action to get on with his transition. Another client, similarly concerned about what she observed in her own workplace, decided after finishing a Phase I visualization project that she should stay put.

---

*For example, see Joseph E. Shorr's fine book *Go See the Movie in Your Head* (New York, Popular Library, 1977).

I'm not completely thrilled about what's happening in this company, but know now that this is my best, present alternative. I need another year or two in this position before jumping ship.

If after Phase I tasks we are still hazy about our goals, we can explore Phase II's potential more deeply. Some of these projects might include:

- locating and observing fictional (or real-life) role models who live the solutions we think we want;
- writing out our reactions to these models, especially noticing what we think, say and do to hold ourselves back from these same outcomes or how we idealize their "perfect" lives, while discounting ours;
- examining the mood, feelings or experience of our goal as it relates to our actual way of being, our current experience and the context of our life today;
- building elementary written composites of our solutions (e.g., with short vivid paragraphs, we can describe the working world we hope to enter).

Many popular books and seminars can help us through these early explorations,* although later, as I've stressed, we should try to stay on our own. Independently, we can teach ourselves "how" to catch on while also instilling true absorption in ourselves. It is this fascination, this solitary and quite prudent, low-risk quest, that makes our eye single, lets us mentally dance with our possibilities or potential answers and moves us from our ordinary mind into insight.

Someone like Ben can write a short story whose plot involves him directly as a hero doing the work he wants in the way he wants. This writing stimulates and imprints consciousness, lets one see the routes to new goals or success in a way that mere linear thinking cannot do.

Others might want to keep a "mental scrapbook" during the ordinary working day, noticing and mentally snapping images of situations that have great emotional appeal. Then, at night, before falling asleep,

---

*For instance, see any of Neville's works or Catherine Ponder's *Open Your Mind to Prosperity.* One of the more novel, newer systems especially related to money issues is Dr. John Kappas's "Mental Bank" Program (available from the Panorama Publishing Company, Van Nuys, CA 91411).

when most relaxed, they can review these pictures in short, vivid scenarios, inserting themselves into each frame, actually feeling themselves in the desirable circumstance. In a peaceful, unhurried, noncompetitive climate, in all safety and with complete trust and guilelessness, we imaginatively reinvent our circumstances. Thus, we take our attention *off* our problem and engage ourselves fully with solutions. The old adage "What you focus on you get" fits here.

Our reinvention work has no stiff guidelines. We accept and grow easy with the notion that *there is no one way.* We explore and befriend our own ways, ideas and feelings. All these will vary from time to time. As we mature and develop, our habits and emotions may very well change, too. I repeat these points in order to stress and reinforce them; it is easy to expect perfection or to try to conform ourselves to what we think is an idealized standard.

By taking our preferred ways seriously yet holding lightly the general, overall process, we give ourselves permission to be silly or dull-witted, or quick or slow. This seems the very indulgence that dissolves our uncreative barriers. We erected these ourselves as early strategic defenses against the force, brutality, insensitivities or dominance of others. If, for instance, as children we were expected always to be neat, to succeed, to "master" or control ourselves in the stringent way parents or elders saw fit, we may have adopted beliefs, a worldview or actions that now limit us. Children who quickly stifled their finest instincts with perfectionism in order to please others may have forbidden themselves mistakes, flaws, illness, a fantasy life. As adults, they can just as easily forgo needed recreation, or distrust opportunities to daydream or thwart their own knowledge of what it means to take healthy, quite normal and completely necessary rest. Sometimes such adults can only relax by getting sick! Much willfulness and resistance seems to be a way to defend against this attack on self. Now, through safe, private, mental, experiential or actual play, we have an alternative—can gently recover our soft side, our inventiveness, our truly resourceful selves. Positive Structuring provides this chance.*

Phase II means we enter the spirit of our objective, understanding its mood, tone or appearance. Remember that Positive Structuring is simply adult *play*—if we grow tired of it, or feel no desire to continue, we simply stop. In Ben's case, Phase III play was totally unnecessary,

---

*For an overview of the rudiments of play, see Louis C. Andros's book *Play: The Intentional Avoidance of Work* (POB 234, Scotts Mills, OR 97375). Andros reminds us that recovering our ability to play starts with converting "work" into spontaneous, effortless adventure.

since the first two stages of activities produced concrete information. Ben knew what he wanted to do and proceeded. But sometimes we still aren't certain. Then Phase III's model building helps us take low-risk, practical actions that bring some minimal part of our objective into being. It is this tangible step that seems to be so informative and self-corrective. Often, for instance, the imaging tasks of the first phases of any change technique produce idealized or grandiose notions of the goal. People who merely engage in visualization exercises often report falling into this "glamorous trap." If we test ourselves in some tangible way in the arena of our objective, we are likely to know firsthand if we want to continue. Then too, even when we have clearly identified our objective, our own fears of actualizing it can confuse us. A woman who clung to what she called her "toxic boyfriend" said, "If I give him up, I'll have to learn real intimacy. This terrifies me." Creating small physical or experiential models of what we want can thus order and clarify what we're feeling and lead us more gradually, adventuresomely toward a better life.

Phase III: Solution Architecture—Creating a Model

One of my own playful experiments might shed light on this method. More than a decade ago, I began toying with the idea of leaving a secure, tenured position in public-sector management. I wanted to found my own business, but feared I could not successfully function alone. A chief concern was whether or not I could comfortably relinquish my role as a community leader. I loved the responsibilities of my public-sector job and enjoyed being recognized as a leader in a first-rate school, district and organization. The management team with which I worked was one of the best and most progressive nationwide. All this seemed a lot to give up on a whim.

Though my original career goal had been to become a school superintendent, soon after I was made a school principal, I saw that the superintendent's position might not fit me or be fulfilling. Nevertheless, I worried that I might regret moving into private industry. Leaving seemed too high a risk to take without more feedback and data. I designed a project for myself (at the time, I called it "research," not Positive Structuring) to determine how uncomfortable—or comfortable—an independent, nontraditional job would be. My first objective was simply to determine if I could survive a worst-case possibility—

namely, having to take *any* job just to make financial ends meet while waiting for my entrepreneurial projects to produce a viable income. With this in mind, I found a weekend job as a waitress at a health-food bar in Malibu, California. My new work was perfectly wholesome, and I worked in gorgeous surroundings with Beautiful People as customers. The tasks were totally foreign to me, and at first I felt quite homesick and strange. Of course, I continued with my profession during the week, but still felt ill at ease. Each weekend I gained firsthand knowledge of what it would *feel* like to leave my familiar, secure setting— where I had mentors, status, belonging and credibility—and begin anew.

In a few weeks, I was enjoying my new part-time work. Although it was intellectually less satisfying and much more physically demanding than I'd expected, I quickly saw that it was not so much the title or power of school superintendent, principal or professor I wanted, but the opportunity to use what I sensed were natural leadership and communication abilities. After two or three months as a weekend waitress, I was made manager of the kitchen. Again, I received feedback through direct experience of my real interests, talents and vocational needs. Again, I related these needs more to communication and leadership drives than to status or power. Apparently, in the kitchen or classroom, I would exert influence. As soon as this was clear, and immediately upon discovering I *could* survive my worst-case, low-income scenario, I resigned from both jobs, fully confident I could make it on my own whatever the setting.

Waitressing gave me insight about my vocational needs. I required challenge, not status, and a chance to contribute to the large-scale upgrading of individual and group functioning. To this day, I am careful never to deny myself leadership opportunities, or personal or professional creative freedom, and have declined senior management positions in excellent but bureaucratic industries as a result of that concrete "study model."

LIFE IS NOT A GUIDED TOUR

Those who seek security, fringe benefits or the approval and praise of authority figures—certainly those who wonder, "What will people think?"—are sometimes loath to engage in this kind of hands-on experimental inquiry. Clearly, this "play" is not for everyone. And who can tell us what exact line of inquiry will produce maximum information for *us*? If we hope to actively alter the course of our lives, there are no blueprints for what to do. However, each of us can experiment if we are serious about trying things another way.

I recently read a quote posted above a career counselor's desk. A retired man had written her a note, which I paraphrase:

> Those who continue to grow, despite their age, are always in a continuous state of gearing up for life's next challenge. They maintain a forward momentum and are infectiously enthused about life— which is, after all, an adventure, not a guided tour.

As long as we worry about what people will say or lean indiscriminantly on others for a way out of trouble, we remain powerless when familiar work, family or personal systems change. The most common examples are the anxiety, anger and helplessness that workers feel when their companies announce upcoming mergers, or the rage and victimization that one spouse feels when the other wants to go a different way in life. Similarly, people get angry at Positive Structuring itself—usually at the method—because it consists of necessarily vague tasks that lack specific direction. Clients either give up or demand I tell them "how" to design their models. They study my expressions for approval about their journal entries. They seek out colleagues and friends with whom they can compare notes. Then, realizing this is counterproductive, they can become sullen or resentful. I have warned seminar attendees of the futility of trivializing their self-improvement projects or ambitions by exposing these prematurely to superficial conversations or to the merely curious scrutiny of others. People who succeed at Positive Structuring learn that self-understanding and inventiveness come only with time and courage. Those who cannot tolerate frustration, who cannot wait for answers, those who become anxious when immediate direction is not forthcoming, those who lack training in the steady hunt for one-of-a-kind answers, can feel betrayed. Still, Positive Structuring seems worth our time because most of us won't have much choice about whether or not we make a transition into novel living, work or relationship arrangements. I recently read a startling figure about the decline of the U.S. middle class. Although the number of high income earners has increased (households of $60,000 per year or more have gone from 8 percent to 13 percent in twenty years), those middle-class families with low or average yearly incomes have shrunk. (Naisbitt, 1990) For many, the issue now becomes how well can we create, time and take our moves?

Some people experience overwhelming anxiety when changes are announced. A story in the *Wall Street Journal* (Bennett, 1988) reported feedback from several focus groups of large-company managers. When asked how the corporate restructurings of the previous few years affected their attitudes toward their jobs, many expressed continued emotional upset from the turmoil of these disruptions. They viewed their employers as the enemy. Beneath their understandable emotion about now-unemployed colleagues, was an unexpressed longing for protection, guarantees and security. Those interviewed reported they originally went to work for their companies because of job security, fringe benefits and profit sharing. Sounding much like the executives I quote in Chapter 1, these managers want no entrepreneurial risks.

Yet learning to accommodate *moderate* risk is precisely the skill that alleviates anxieties during sudden change. Positive Structuring helps us learn to take chances without shooting ourselves in the foot, simply because it forces us to move easily, slowly and responsibly toward our goals or through transitions. As we grow more self-confident, we also become anchors or stabilizers for others—our spouses, families, children or work-mates. Then we project a truthful, humane self-assurance that touches others and comforts and instructs.

For instance, managers able to tolerate the ambiguity of corporate transitions find they can motivate and inspire both themselves *and* others during rapid organizational change. They can concentrate and work despite very real professional concerns or uncertainty. These managers emerge from the crises as stronger and more capable people. Certainly, this is true not just of managers in business but of individuals in every walk of life. Feelings of powerlessness, the sense that we have "lost control" and weakened self-confidence are normal states for those of us who have not, or who cannot, work through unstable circumstances.

GROWING COMFORTABLE WITH CHAOS: CULTIVATING TRUE INTELLIGENCE

Those who tolerate uncertainty easily admit to discomfort, fearful moments and weaknesses. This very self-acceptance lets them cope with their emotions, giving them a flexible edge or advantage not available to rigid, ever-in-control types who exist in a state of denial. For example, CD, the biophysicist mentioned earlier, believes he has become self-confident by his "disciplined remembering" that life presents a cycle of ups and downs. CD's experience with uncertainty, his memory of his own defeats and successes, bolsters his creative adaptation in his current circumstance:

My confidence in the face of the unknown may relate to my life's experience. There is an inevitable cycle in youth that dampens creative output—a time when one doesn't "know," flails about, is confused.

When we are young—say, in early childhood—most of us are enthusiastic creators. Then, whatever our eventual work—even if we don't attend college—we enter a period of accumulating knowledge. This is a time when creativity seems suppressed. We are building a knowledge or experience base, finding out what works and what doesn't, soaking up all kinds of data. Here is when we don't have all the answers.

Later, when we have amassed our knowledge base, we can *apply* what we know to specific work or personal problems. But we have to remember to come out of ourselves and be creative again, as we were when we were children. If we can remember ourselves as we were in early childhood, we often gain confidence or solve problems in our own way and thus move through the unknown more boldly— to find answers of our own. If we can recall how it was *not* to know, and realize we survived, we can apply that memory to our present unknowns.

When I first began solving problems in this way, I saw myself repeating what others before me had done. Even though my answers seemed repetitious, I gained courage—it was comforting to know that my mind worked along lines that I respected. After a while it became second nature to think independently, and with this a feeling of power ensued.

CD has learned that everything—"good" and "bad"—is useful to one's growth and autonomy. Creative adaptors are renewed by their own response style, continually regenerated in an organic, holistic and natural way. "I know I can't control externals," said one man, "so I work on staying flexible—when I say I *work* on it, I mean it's an ongoing lesson." Such persons flow with the movement of larger, interactive systems like nature, social systems or family, feeling themselves integrally connected with these systems, and seeing the systems themselves as synergistic or coherent. Without elaborate study or explanation, these things make sense. They feel linked somehow either to others' thought processes, to a body of knowledge or to an active, interrelated universal order. They land on their feet appropriately when they must, but don't know "how" to meet change, largely because of the resiliency of their perceptions.

As I have suggested, this common ground or sense of continuity and belonging stems from a universal mind-set or heightened consciousness. This elevated awareness (or unity) has a psychosocial influence on everyone who experiences it. It moves us toward greater subjective health, inventiveness and autonomy. Moreover, the unitive influence is obvious when people live—don't just talk—their highest values or are faithful to the law of their own being.

Through whatever means we arrive at this state, those who report growing comfort with change, disorder and personal transitions say this ability stems from their increased interior stability, order and reliability. Alertness, mindfulness or wakefulness, clarity of perceptions and inner peace can become a "normal" way of being. For most, interior calm may not be constant, but will at least be known and trusted when the individual feels disrupted. Such a person will feel his or her personal strength as a natural center, way or condition. Fear, turmoil and all the unsettled feelings born of insecurity, alienation and dependencies are experienced as "not really me." Over time, these disruptive feelings lessen, while inner calm, self-mastery and the ability to be enthused or absorbed increase.

Although we have been taught to believe that creative people are generally neurotic or temperamentally strange, we may have been instructed by those who were themselves neurotic or temperamentally strange. Little is known about emotionally healthy creatives. They may truly be a different breed. They live responsible, vitally connected, productive lives because their creativity is an ongoing, adaptive, dialectical process by which they themselves come into being. We are just learning what this human potential involves and know little about how it is developed.

Many paths lead us to our own creative powers, though intense absorption seems a must. A task, hobby, relationship, meditation, se-lected physical disciplines—all can open the way if approached with disciplined, committed action.

Creative adaptives are excited by their power to live fully and well. To the extent that they gain an awareness of something greater, their external resourcefulness is strengthened. One long-term practitioner of TM reported this experience:

> I am no longer overwhelmed by people or my environment. My ease is greater or I could say I feel somehow bigger. My perceptions become sharper, more refined, and problems don't make such a deep impression on me—they pass into my sphere, I handle them and they move out of my life. Handling what's in front of me is fun.

A friend spent two weeks at a nondenominational, silent retreat. She spoke about feeling "centered." Sounding much like the long-term mediator, she reported her everyday effectiveness improved by just this short time alone:

> The thing I notice most is how my awareness has sharpened. While I was on retreat, I was tremendously alert or "awake." I felt that the problems I'd come to think about were easy ones—not at all threatening as I'd thought. I felt that I could meet my responsibilities without caving in. I sensed that I had a knack for spontaneous right action.
>
> Now that I'm home, I practice silence and a kind of Zen breathing each morning. That way, each day I touch a bit of that peace I now know lives within me.

Positive Structuring projects can help us enhance this inner comfort, this feeling of connectedness, but not immediately. We have to take time to grow our interests, and to open up to the workings of our mind. The projects themselves become an awakening device. For instance, we can restore feelings of self-confidence by going on wilderness tours, like Audubon nature walks or other outdoor, environmental programs. We can tackle any new hobby where we observe ourselves learning. In all these activities we integrate our various intelligences and watch our resourcefulness. Gradually, we develop respect for our inherent powers. We do not need to meet and conquer every conceivable challenge in order to grow in this way. We only must know ourselves as able in something, see ourselves meet uncertainty once or twice, in order to bring this self-respect to our daily functioning. The Zen saying, "If you can do anything well, you can do everything well," fits here.

IN OUR OWN TIME AND WAY: THE WISDOM OF SELF-OBSERVATION

Just as self-discipline and confidence are necessary correlates to our "enjoyment" of disorder, so, too, as mentioned, is understanding our own mode of creation. More than just accommodating a personal work style, beyond learning patience or discipline in the face of lengthy problem-solving projects, we must *trust* our own way of bringing some new thing into being. This means we identify the thought-patterns contained within our unique process, become intimate observers of ourselves. As suggested, this is meditation and art—even for scientists. CD describes this:

There is an art to every scientist's individual process. For example, some scientists have a good nose for problems. Why is this? Why do some people *know* what to work on while others spend a lifetime wondering?

Knowing what to work on is an intuitive thing, although it is probably one of the most worthwhile things to understand. It is hard to spot one's own way of "knowing," yet each of us has a pattern—if we can find it—that reveals the answer.

CD knows what to work on because his "catching-on" skills are well developed. Along these same lines, Ben Shahn wrote that the discovery of images and the recognition of shapes and forms *is* the process of art, and that these awaken a response that seems to be peculiar to us. (Morse, 1972) I propose that Positive Structuring can help each of us discover our own specific thought-forms, "see" the shapes and patterns of our creative process. This integrative learning bolsters our belief in ourselves as both catalysts and as people who can change. Within our individuated thought and discovery processes are housed the very systems of inquiry we can use to solve all problems. To locate our personal discovery process, we might ask ourselves:

- How have I solved my most serious life-problems in the past? (i.e., what thought/action *process* did I use?)
- What kinds of problems do I typically enjoy solving, and how do I come at my solutions during those times when I "play" with answers?
- When I am not sure what to do, what do I notice myself doing in order to find my way? What seem to be my most productive thought patterns? What's least helpful?
- If I were teaching a small child "how" to survive a crisis or how to cope with the unknown, what would my primary, most basic lessons be?
- How—by what conservative, *gentle* methods—would I teach a child (whom I loved) to creatively adapt? To be resourceful? To be self-observing?
- How resourceful were my parents? My teachers? What did I learn about creative problem-solving from them?
- Whom do I know, work with or see regularly whose creativity I don't admire? What attributes, behaviors or traits do they have that I share?
- Whom do I know, work with or see regularly whose creativity I admire? What attitudes, behaviors or traits does this person have that I might copy, borrow, develop?

By asking ourselves such questions, we may discover one pattern or cycle within another. Our answers can lead us to design small, low-risk Positive Structuring projects of our own. For example, one woman noticed her best ideas came while she took long walks. She made a study model out of this by writing down work-related questions each evening before she went for her walk and took a minicassette to capture her answers. In time, because this proved so successful for her, she incorporated this habit into her life: "It's like brushing my teeth. I don't feel right if I forget to record my answers and ideas during or after a walk." (Others use their dreams in much the same way.) One man, on realizing that he had a poor track record as a solution-finder, designed small, low-risk study models that involved progressively more difficult puzzles. Because he liked word games, he took himself through a series of these, each one more difficult than the last. While he played, he observed his mind's workings. In a few months, he grew in self-respect: "If my brain can figure out these anagrams, there's no reason why I can't use this same mind in my regular life."

OUR OWN HEROIC ADVENTURE: PATTERN REVEALS PURPOSE

As we review our answers to the open-ended questions we pose for ourselves, our pattern of resolution is revealed to us.*

In other words, our *way* of solving problems contains repeating elements of our life's central motif. If we can determine what this way is, our peculiar, thoroughly unique problem-solving history will become readily apparent. The archetypical theme, or heroic aspect, of our particular existence becomes discernable, and this "theme" is unique, even though aspects of it are also quite universal and shared by others. Do we, for instance, feel ourselves to be adventurers or warriors? Do we approach matters as do certain great men or women about whom we've read? Do we see ourselves as victims and martyrs or as rescuers? Each of these major types has specific characteristics and life-scripts. To gain clarity about our life's themes, we can give firm direction to an otherwise meandering, nonspecific journey.

Key day-to-day troubles, irritations, problems and even solution styles also hold clues about our life's central theme. One person is always in a rush, and has the dominant sense that there's not enough time. Another irritates family and friends by crawling along or resisting, withholding. If we are privy to the latter's personal problems, we may learn he or she is sexually dysfunctional along these same withholding lines: if a man, he may be impotent; if a woman, frigid. Stepping back, looking at our life through this wide-angle lens, we may spot repeating conflicts, compulsions or even heartbreaking, recurring weaknesses. These repetitions hold messages that tell us about our soul's deeply seated hurts, fears or traumas. If we learn to speak this subtle language, we can interpret what is needed for liberation, autonomy and real personal power.

---

*In fact, our individual way of solving problems may consist of both a favorite *process* and *themes* or issues (however hidden). We may spot micro/macro cycles with the general patterns of our life.

By resolving everyday tensions, by objectively observing ourselves, we can restructure our internal codes, cues and psychic motifs. Positive Structuring exercises—the models, for instance— let us build small, restructuring experiences. Through these we uncover, then solve, the primary dilemmas of our existence. For instance, I discovered my true vocational needs through a "pretend" work experience that let me safely view a basic, underlying fear within myself. The job was real, but I used it as a simulation to explore deeper issues of my vulnerability, my humanity, my life's ambitions. These ambitions, or drives, were strong ones, but prior to my experiment I never fully understood the power of my fear, never really knew what called me. My employment "adventure" taught me, firsthand, what only I could learn.

Anyone can discover his or her life's purpose through similar, low-key experiments. Even our study models and our thinking patterns carry messages, reveal our limits, our talents and our deepest mission. Most of us are completely unaware that our problem-solving motif holds clues to the character and theme of our entire existence. But highly creative people somehow do spot connections between their ordinary concerns, their creative process and the metaphors, symbols or struggles that underscore their life's heroic adventure. For instance, the artist SW discussed her problem-solving patterns:

> A friend and I compared notes about our backgrounds and our current creative competencies. Our backgrounds are completely opposite. I was raised in a protected but sometimes violently abusive family, where I wasn't ever given the opportunity to express my ideas.
>
> My friend's mother—an alcoholic who loved her, but who leaned on her from the earliest age as if she (the daughter) was the mother— turned to her daughter for support and often for solutions to family problems.
>
> As an adult, I often had trouble trusting my opinions in decision-making, (except in my art) and when I had to make my own way in life (at age eighteen) my initial pattern was to grope for solutions and feel anxious. I had to teach myself that my decisions were valid. On the other hand, my friend always approaches problem-solving with ease. She rarely questions her own judgment.

As a young adult, SW strove to value herself and her decision-making abilities. These are, in fact, ample. Her central concern was her search for ways to build self-worth and trust. SW now realizes that this personal quest for self-value also drove her artistic efforts:

> At least I could communicate through pictures. In time, I found intense need to communicate through words. Thus I began to write, first in my journal and then to people who inspired me, who touched my life in some way. All this has built my positive self-regard.

Others invariably have different patterns that naturally represent other life-concerns. In all cases, the cycle of our problem-solving can instruct us. It has distinctive, multiple energies: now we are confused, frenetic and disorderly. Now intense, focused and uniquely self-disciplined. Now active and driving. Soon passive or classically meditative. Finally, we grow insightful, orderly, coherent, as our problem is resolved. Out of our individualized, dynamic, intense involvement with a problem—what Rollo May, in his book *The Courage to Create,* calls absorbed engagement—comes more than just isolated answers. Our whole life can be furthered in some purposeful way *if* we *use* problems to grow self-aware about our creative process.

May concludes that consciousness itself is born out of true creative acts, out of the knowing/not-knowing struggle of creation. Indeed, this does seem so. In her book *Notebooks of the Mind,* Vera John-Steiner quotes the scholar Howard E. Gruber, who describes each creative life as existing within a larger creative cycle:

> A creative moment is part of a longer creative process, which in its turn is part of a creative life. How are such lives lived? How can I express this peculiar idea that such an individual must be a self-generating system? Not a system that comes to rest when it has done good work, but one that urges itself onward. And yet, not a run away system that accelerates its activity to the point where it burns itself out in one flash. The system regulates the activity and the creative acts regenerate the system. The creative life happens in a being who can continue to work. (John-Steiner, 1987, p.78)

On the simplest, perhaps most obvious level, I suggest that our typical response to problems holds a message about our life's motif or central drive. CD admits this was the case in his own life. In early life, he wanted to understand science as it related to the medical field. This seemed his life's sole quest, much as SW yearned to build self-trust and decision-making power. In college and after graduate school, CD studied the relationship between certain protein molecules and muscle and nerve diseases. He "pushed back the science a bit," but in time left medical research for a job in the food industry. Now, some five years later, CD finds himself working on sleep disorders, researching the way in which milk and other food products affect sleep patterns:

> I am intensely interested in the same issues that called to me early in my professional life—incrementally I seem to be satisfying my lifelong interest in medicine. I feel my vocation has been consistent, even though, on superficial levels, I've changed fields.
>
> On another frontier of creative interest, my hobby is photography. The photographs I most enjoy are those taken with a close-up lens. I like to get in close. I love taking microscopically exact pictures, see the patterns, shapes and colors of flowers or plants and find out what these are saying to me.

CD's photography, his work and his idiosyncratic problem-solving process provide a consistent, whole fabric of related patterns. These reflect a message about what matters to him, about his motives, drives and the particular, intrinsic satisfactions of his life. To know ourselves in this way, to interpret our own nonconscious messages, seems a key to living a self-aware, fulfilled life. Many projects can help us build this skill.

To strengthen our interpretive muscles, we could design a small study model to decode our dreams. Instead of merely logging our dreams each night to search for their psychological message, we might record them for lengthy periods, to try to identify one or two recurring themes, conflicts or wishes. In some ways, locating and reading our life's message is much like intelligent dream analysis. Harry Stack Sullivan used to train young analysts to provide patients with at least two interpretations of their dreams. The patients were to choose between them. Their choices conveyed a message. When we interpret our own dreams, we have infinite options from which to select. Our final deciphering gives us information about ourselves. Many dream workshops and texts on dream analysis and certain schools of therapy can help us understand the messages in our dreams. (Delayne, 1979)

Each person's problem-solving process and discovery cycle is peculiarly unique. Thus, dreams, thought-languages, problems, the manner in which we tackle the bulk of our problems, really everything, seems a giant information field, ready to tell us about ourselves. All that's needed is to teach ourselves about our own language. Or invent it.

FOR THE FUN OF IT: OVERCOMING ANXIETY

Why do creative adaptive people find that ordering disorder is so much "fun"? Why does this act hold such magnetic charm for some people? Why might our unique manner of play, our use of leisure time, imagination or problem-solving appeal to us, help us grow?

First, we benefit from disorder when problems that need sorting and ordering are real, meaningful and truthful to us. Related to this is the fact that solutions often bring fulfillment and a release of tension, especially when we reconcile some deep frustrations or resolve a keenly felt injustice or contradiction. Someone who, after years of indecision, finally commits to this or that course of action understands this fact. Writer Brenda Ueland's remark that all prisoners should learn creative writing emphasizes another way in which tensions lessen through active, resourceful ordering, in this case self-expression:

> All prisoners should write. It would be good for them and good for us. Some of the greatest literature has been written by prisoners, among them Sir Walter Raleigh, Bunyan and Dostoevsky.
>
> Prisoners suffer, think and are alone, so they have very much to say. Their creative yearning and power is shown by the fact that there is much more demand for great literature in prisons than outside. (Ueland, 1987, p.116)

Ironically, we can enjoy disorder even when it stimulates anxiety. This is not quite as perverse as it first sounds. By mastering a thing, or simply by fully participating in a dilemma, we confront, then triumph over, early fears of ineptness, abandonment or separation. Fairy tales, myths and "primitive" child-rearing methods typically encouraged youngsters to face their demons, to move boldly toward fears. The notion that we are transformed by accepting our darkest selves, by meeting and embracing our shadow, shame or guilt is universally held.

There is also a well-recognized link between anxiety and the death instinct. For instance, children feel anxious (as do adults) when they face separation, personal loss or the threat of death. An infant feels something close to the fear of dying when separated from its mother. If, for whatever reason, a child does not learn to handle such separation, if he does not discover his own competence, feel himself to be capable of standing on his own as an individuated being, then he easily regresses to earlier states of development. For example, children who learn by attending kindergarten that they can survive, though separated from parents, can then proceed developmentally. They are free to explore ever-larger regions of life independently. Thus from the disorder of fear can come to organizing, freeing lessons.

Anxiety also follows children into adolescence (and then into adulthood) if self-trust and the growth toward autonomy have not been gained along childhood's way. SW's remarks about her need to teach herself how to think independently and validate her own decisions lets us see how these critical attributes help anyone's ability to retain inner balance during stress or times of rapid personal transition.

People with strong creative adaptive responses tend to be self-accepting. Like SW, they accommodate and trust their feelings, even though these might seem at first uncomfortable or unglamorous. Then they "move into," accept or amplify these emotions in order to be who they truly are. For example, SW functions despite unpleasant feelings—not by fighting them but by acknowledging and accommodating them in an orderly fashion, by learning to outgrow these. When we do this prudently, we learn to accept death itself—consciously or not. Since fears of death and anxiety are so closely intertwined, when we accept our fears, we also accept the dark body of experience and emotion that represents death itself.

At that point, we are mysteriously energized and can move with our life instincts despite fear—just as a kindergarten youngster is free to grow developmentally. We look our private forebodings square in the face and vote, with our choices, to live fully. Since we are not using huge stores of energy to suppress what we feel, we gain what it takes to act creatively. Those who strangle their own life because of unacceptable fears deny themselves enormous integrative, interpretive and creative power. Their energy and insights are locked up, busy elsewhere, protecting them from demons.

This act of moving with life is precisely what every capable artist does. He or she integrates conflicting shapes, colors and even discordant realities so as to achieve a unification of image and form. Creative adaptors *unify themselves* in exactly this way by means of their own productive attitudes toward problems, emotions, dreams and "undigested," nonconscious experience.

FINDING OUR PERSONAL DIALECTIC

Finally, there is a personal dialectic at work in those with capable creative adaptive responses. Two opposite forces are at work in us: one moves us toward order, the other away from it. Studying how this tension, this dialectic, manifests itself in our life is an exciting part of self-knowledge. This study takes time. For instance, we can observe our own contradictions: When we first start a relationship, are we willing to sustain the risk of being hurt? Do we go in, toward intimacy, then back away? Do we run later? Do we never take risks with money, only to be trapped in semipoverty because we miss investment opportunities? Does our desire for order and safety cause us to limit ourselves in other ways? Such contradictory impulses interact in such a way that our subsequent reconciliation of tension furthers our entire existence in tangible, and also intangible, ways. In other words, if we can spot this pull, understand what our usual tensions tell us, we can work with, not against, our essential life thrust.

CD's sense that his work choices allow him to address his lifelong interest in medical research illustrates how conflict might be tangibly resolved. The intangible movements of life are harder to describe simply because they involve personal transfiguration of spirit or life-purposes. As SW demonstrates, by attending to and accepting our deepest life-conflicts, then working to resolve them, however cautiously and prudently, we recover our true self.

For each of us, the motifs and problems of our psyche hold answers to the questions of our very existence. We address our life's spiritual—or heroic—quest by creatively attending to practical, quite ordinary problems. We accelerate this spiritual development as well as our creative capabilities by inventing projects that help us study, then solve, problems. Positive Structuring teaches us how we, as distinctive individuals, think. It helps us contemplate our mind's subtlest faculties. We watch these as we go along, noticing how we predictably order and structure, experience, resist or achieve goals. Initially, we may only learn what we want, may merely identify our objectives. The method cannot progress without this information. Then, as we create study models, we find we must spotlight the particular way in which both tensions and reconciliations germinate from within our consciousness. We cannot advance without grappling with, say, our resistance, our fear of failure or success.

What begins as a vaguely unsatisfying situation soon reveals marvelous bits of information about our ego's needs or our past or our life's central interests, frustrations or mission. Soon we realize that at the start of every problem we structure matters in a particular way. When we reconcile things, we may hold our concern in yet another ideosyncratic fashion. Inevitably, over time we realize that "I am that problem; I am that solution." We are question and answer, depending on our level of awareness. One woman whose life was off-kilter recognized, in time, that when she faced a problem she did so lopsidedly. Another man looked much older than his years and discovered after attending to his thinking that practically every thought was negative, gloomy and weighted down. The influences of our patterned way of thinking are profound: It can help not only our growth but also our health and finances to comprehend in what kind of thought environment we live.

Some call this wisdom. Whatever we choose to call it, we may find that our life is furthered in an elemental, existential way simply by closely, mindfully attending to known and unknown elements. As we order our own chaos—born of the details of daily life—we find ourselves neutralizing long-standing negatives and doing so in a way that dissolves or organizes past ills. The individual whose parents were abusive may find, over time, that escape from lovelessness is not impossible.

Love comes from (and in) the higher mental state. Someone whose parents were impoverished and who was formerly convinced of scarcity may see a way out. Inner affluence begets a luxurious life. People raised to be idle or pampered can someday find themselves called to stewardly roles and might even serve mankind. These are all examples of how new levels of discernment give us power to make use of discord. Each person's intelligent passage into past incoherencies can eventually reveal gentle ways to disengage from an unhelpful past of unwanted programs. This is an inventive process grounded in self-awareness. To me, this is true art with heroic potential.

No wonder there is stimulation, transformation and enjoyment here. This is play of the highest human caliber—the soul enlarging itself, expanding into the depths of its consciousness, inventing new realities in which to play some more.

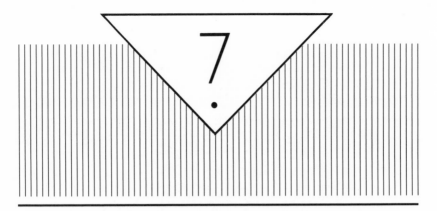

A 21st-CENTURY MIND IS VISIONARY

He who has a why to live can bear most any how.

NIETZSCHE

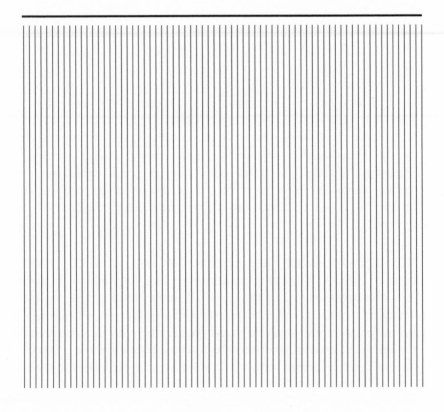

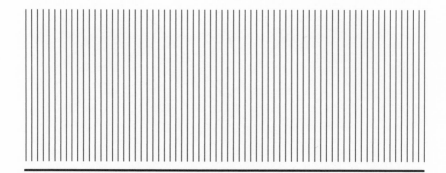

The great sculptor Henry Moore once remarked that Michelangelo's monumental vision was discernible even in his thumbnail-sized sketches. Moore believed that enormity of vision was embedded in the artist's imagination—not in the size of his creation. So it seems with us: Our dream of life—when we have it—permeates our very being. But why is it that some of us feel so certain of our directions while others spend a lifetime wondering why they exist?

The spiritually mature know their place in the larger scheme of things and realize what force it is that moves them. Martin Buber wrote that beneath and behind each person's feeling of destiny lies a deeply experienced subjective power, drive or direction:

> The commotion of our human life . . . is closed only to *one* thing: unity. . . . The soul that has tensed itself utterly to burst through the commotion and escape from it is the soul that receives the grace of unity. Whether the soul meets a loved human being, or a wild landscape of heaped-up stones—from this being, this heap of stones, grace catches fire [and the soul] . . . experiences unity, the world: itself. All its powers come into play. (Buber, 1985, p.2)

Those who sense their destiny in an intense way are like moths drawn to a flame. They may somehow be better connected to their deepest consciousness and thus yearn to express this inexpressible something in whatever way possible—through work, art, relationship, leadership, community service or even war. Their sacrificial stance is often palpable: parents, artists, teachers, statespersons and those in religious or military service reveal themselves to us as leaders to be reckoned with when they have, in Nietzsche's words, "a why to live."

When people's minds are touched by the unitive sense, they feel as if, to use the words of Saint John of the Cross, they have been infused with a "seed of fire."

Although we often feel that a life's dream must be large if it is to be at all, this just isn't so. Those who desire conventional things—to be good parents and have warm, nurturing family lives; to experience financial stability, committed, loving marriages or personal fulfillment—may have great vision. In the face of present-day realities, as we try to read our futures, the unclear path presented by major worldwide problems is apparent. Whether we examine the way that superindustrial powers' growth will effect our environment or think about our planet's prospect for true, long-term peace, the simple wish for a harmonious, stable personal life seems heroic. This goal may not be as easy to get as it once was. However down-to-earth our aims sound, if we hope for a life rich with humane or spiritual qualities, we have vision. Moreover, with vision even an unclear, thorny path is easier to travel than without it.

Part of the difficulty in owning a personal vision may come from the word *vision* itself. We typically think that this means we must have impressive dreams or be motivated by a grandiose plan. Unitive consciousness is grand enough in itself. When this high awareness is the context in which we hold or see our life's objectives, the most modest goals become enlivened.

Of course, some people do "think big," feel deeply and have exciting future plans. Many factors produce large dreams. Talents press to be used. The more talent we possess, the likelier it is that we feel compelled to dispense it widely. Injustices and social ills can generate such intense emotions that sometimes these wake us up, urge us on, ask us to surpass ourselves. We sense there is something we must do in life, even to the point of sacrificing our comforts or ourselves. Martin Luther King's assassination, the deaths of President and Bobby Kennedy, the more recent demonstrations and mass killings in China and Romania, the destruction of the Berlin Wall, pictures of moon landings, the AIDS epidemic, rain forests in peril or the greenhouse effect—any external circumstances can move us, remind us of what we need to do or must do with our lives in order to have lived well or honor our values. Altruism stirs vision. People who join the Peace Corps or enter other low-paying but personally rewarding professions are usually ablaze with high ideals. Many are incredibly motivated to accomplish some hard-to-name, indescribable good, and not a few are frustrated because they find no ready outlet for these motives.

To begin understanding our own vision, we can ask ourselves if there were ever events that touched us so deeply that we made a vow about how we wanted to spend our life. For example, as children or teenagers, perhaps we encountered some abuse, trauma or unfairness, and then said to ourselves, "If it takes the rest of my life, I'm going to remedy this injustice." Or maybe we lived through a political tragedy that moved us to the point that we then wondered how we might contribute to the solution, and thereby make a difference. Such happenings can remind us of our purposes, help us see why we are around. Our answers need not be profound or "significant"; they can be inconsequential, ordinary thoughts that point to our true aims.

WE KNOW WHEN WE DON'T HAVE IT

While we may not always empathize with, or appreciate, someone else's dream, we usually know when we ourselves lack direction. People who are hard-pressed to find meaning in life usually experience "quiet desperation." I caution those who ask what they must do to find their vision not to put the cart before the horse. We should first seek our deepest core, the Kingdom within; then all else will be clear to us. If we, or if society or a group, has no central purpose, morale plummets. Lionel Tiger's fine book *Optimism* demonstrates that cultures that endure are those with optimistic belief systems. These groups believe in the worth, value of and possibilities their own futures. As individuals, so must we.

America is fortunate to have had, from its inception, a societal vision. When Europeans speak of Americans, whatever flaws are mentioned, they regularly comment on our energy, high motivation and pragmatic, take-action qualities. In part we are an energized people because we have inherited the dreams and processes of democracy and a heterogenous, free people who strive to make this dream a reality.

Perhaps vision is most readily observable when we examine the business world. We notice a leader's foresight, or watch corporations— like Chrysler in the eighties—pull themselves together, cohesively move away from problematic conditions and toward increasingly healthy, productive states. We attribute these results largely to a leader's "vision." But we seldom notice that parents, teachers, craftspersons—*any* conscious, active person with imagination—can also embody leadership and vision. Then they usually motivate themselves as well as others. When anyone, of any age or background, has an image of what's possible, he or she can instill that same idea in others. Vision is infectious.

Managers in mediocre businesses can stimulate their groups to produce quality workmanship and exhibit enthusiasm, high morale and perseverance. Coaches with vision for their athletes' potential inspire unbelievable effort and achievement. Scientists and technicians who team up to send astronauts into space, families who band together to overcome hardship or illness, experience firsthand the importance of these deeply felt intrinsic drives.

If we were to visit any viable, thriving business (whether it employs one person or thirty thousand), we would find large dreams behind the firm's prosperity. For many years, I have worked with one of the world's major consumer product companies. I've observed its employees go through numerous changes, some quite massive and dramatic. Through good times and anxious ones, the collectively held, corporate value of producing high-quality products has lasted. Employees cling to that single notion as everything else familiar fades from sight. Corporations that lack visionary leaders, an understandable, exciting mission or a history of shared values seemed doomed.

As we develop into whole persons, our vision develops, too. Each of us can accomplish the maximum good through our personal evolution. For instance, I heard of one man who'd accumulated sufficient capital so that he never had to work again. But he realized that he had the ability to use his company as a tool for productive social action and became preoccupied with the environment. When he saw how industrial wastes were contaminating water supplies, he committed a huge percentage of his company's profits to improve matters. Today the bulk of his profits go to environmental causes. Reflecting on his career observers find continuity: this man has always used his business efforts as a social tool; as profitability improved, as his awareness grew, so did his ability to extend his stewardly reach.

VISIONS BIG AND SMALL

Those with creative adaptive skills actualize their long-range life goals incrementally—in their personal lives and their careers. Generally, both areas are upgraded by the person's unique images of what can be done. Just as businesspersons believe they can use their profits as a tool,

creative adaptors in other fields employ their talents, work or community life as a means to help them build the world they value. Underlying
everything such persons hope to accomplish is a broad sense of what
is beneficial and desirable to them and others. This conception heats up
individual purpose and motivation in the same way a corporate leader's
vision motivates others, brings out their best and attracts high-level
talent.

Countless smaller, yet no less important, personal goals exist. To
someone who may not have had a home as a child, home ownership has
great significance. If, in the person's early environment, home ownership was impossible, this objective can become a family-held dream.
Perhaps you strive to be the first one in your family to own your own
business or graduate from college. These aspirations have little to do
with accumulating money and much to do with the triumph of the
human spirit. Such purposes have enormous power to rouse us from
bed each morning.

Whether our personal dream is monumental or human-sized is insignificant. Visions motivate us, stir us to action when these come from
the heart, and all the more so when we are growing creatively. Then
readily we see that we are not so much "achieving," but rather simply
expressing, unfolding, what we already are.

OUR OWN INTRINSIC VISION

How, then, can we live so that our vision belongs to us in some
essential, elemental fashion? How might we grow more into our own,
as complete persons, and live out our distinctive notions of what is
possible? Often the sheer necessities, or repeated frustrations, of our life
show us what we must have. "I deserve better," said a client who'd been
passed over more than once for a long-coveted job. Within a month,
he'd found another position.

One woman whom I interviewed was told—over a decade ago—she
had a life-threatening disease. She feared she would die. She was a
single mother and knew her life's work was not finished. Her daughter
was only sixteen, and she was determined to complete her parenting
role. She resolved to live out her days in good health so that she could
care for her child properly. This was her vision. Today, alive and well,
she continues her work and lives as she intended. Both of these peo-

ple—the executive and the single mother—actualized their vision by reaching out with commitment for what they sensed they deserved.

By contrast, a highly paid executive described his lingering depression. As a young man, he had yearned to be an artist, but his parents ridiculed this goal. Being young and impressionable, he acquiesced to their wishes and instead enrolled in business school. Although he now earns well over a quarter-million dollars yearly, he cannot shake the feeling that something important is missing from his life. This man contemplates suicide, has seen the country's best psychiatrists and exists on tranquilizers. He believes nothing can alleviate his torment. He buried his boyhood vision years ago, yet an unexpressed, persistent dream still haunts him. This longing seeks outlet. Small wonder he cannot find peace or joy. In just this way, millions of people have personal destinies—ideas of what their lives could and should be—and these notions, whether or not realized, are enormously powerful if only in a private way.

Our faith in what is possible brings deep, abiding life-purpose, provides a sense of identity. As we have seen, purposefulness makes it easier to move artfully through life's twists and turns.

Our worldview is molded by our self-perception and our inner world: more than providing happiness, deeper than mere self-interest, vision gives us energy, a spirited sense of why we're here and what we should be doing with our time. Physical or cultural limitations, the lack of education, even conflicting pulls within us, can stimulate great creative adaptive power when our imagination creates a faith in what might be, when we tap into our deepest reserves for our life's mission.

FINDING LIFE'S PURPOSE

What if we lack purpose? In some of us, instinctual life impulses are very weak. Perhaps when we compare ourselves to others who seem to live vigorously, whose inner message for their existence is clear and fully known to them, we feel acute pain or depression. Lack of role models, habit, a tendency to repress our reality or insight, fear of the freedom that we may need (should we identify what we want) can make us far less ambitious or spiritual than we sense we could be. "I can't live up to my own high expectations," said one woman, "so I guess I won't even try." By contrast, an eighteen-year-old who plans to be a cowboy wrote to say he was heading west to get his first job on a dude ranch.

How, then, might adults who are resigned to their unfulfilled lives start, or rekindle, this spark? First, it seems critical not to be too specific or clear when thinking about this issue. Exactitude is often part of our problem. A precise, idealized picture held rigidly in mind will not lead us fruitfully; such images are generally too small, frozen and finite. The narrow specificity of certain externally imposed purposes (such as living out our parents' dream or trying to prove ourselves to others) may severely limit us. These mind-pictures usually are fantasies—self-sabotaging ambitions. These lack rich unconscious information or relevant unresolved questions, are insufficiently powerful to motivate a lifetime's tasks productively. When properly abstract or global, our vision links us to a hero's journey, or to certain deep archetypal energies and drives. These fire us up, keep us growing. As we move toward these important, intrinsic horizons, we conquer ourselves. As we begin to define our long-range goals, it is initially important not to overconcretize our life's dreams. We gain incentive and power when we feel our psychic forces, "hear" the decisive message from within ourselves or find—in the world, in literature, myths, dreams, art, theater and so forth—examples of values, expressions or energies that inspire, touch us deeply, help us reveal our true selves. The Positive Structuring processes can assist our inquiry because this is profoundly spiritual work. The Search helps us pay attention to the stuff of our nonconscious. We begin to understand that life's "vision" is wrapped up tightly with our vocation and identity as persons. When we know who we are, when we understand the context, the particular texture, tone and values of our life—lo and behold—we find our worthwhile purposes.

We know we are on track *either* when we are inwardly peaceful or healthily disturbed. By this I mean if we know we are unhappy about some social injustice, or feel that unresolved personal business demands correction, we can use our awareness as a spotlight to show us what we require. Creative adaptive, self-actualizing or individuated people are not "happy" *all* the time. Like artists, scientists, poets, writers or entrepreneurs who often perceive problems, needs or injustices that they then strive to remedy, describe or resolve in their subsequent work, so it is with us. Our conflicts can inform us—if we stay awake.

We can ask ourselves the following sorts of questions, being careful not to push ourselves to an answer but rather, to let our answers arise from within, in their own way and time:

- What typically disturbs me or moves me—in myself, or in the world? How do I interpret the pattern, or motif, of my upsets? Who do I admire that seems to feel the same way?
- When am I most energized? How purposeful am I as a rule? Who do I see (about whom have I read or heard) who reminds me of a life worth living?
- How enthused about my future am I? Am I excited to greet the next decades, or does this thought frighten, depress or anger me? What would I have to be or do to feel optimistic about the years ahead of me?
- Do I feel life is meaningful? Despite pain, problems and heartaches, am I glad to be alive? If not, are there particular solutions that—if I could address myself to locating these—might remedy my despair?
- Do I experience myself "getting someplace"? Can I describe what I would have to do to feel fulfilled just as I am now? "Where" would I have to get—what would I have to be, do or have—to feel satisfied? Do I want this? Do I prefer adventure, ever moving out—further into the unknown? If so, what sort of adventure predictably fulfills me?
- Do I feel a sense of completion upon attaining my various objectives? Am I always running after illusory goals? Or, at times, do I feel content with things just as they are?
- Do I have a spiritual life and does this life—however I define it—help me know "how" to live? If not, what must I do to develop my spirituality? What does this concept mean to me? Are there other ways to express and describe my highest integrity and overarching life directions?

We know we have purpose when we ourselves are inspired and when others are uplifted, or somehow advanced, by our accomplishments. If after we achieve our goals (e.g., buy a home, finish school, start our business) we experience a sense of completion or feel, "Ah, this is great. I'm glad for this—it was worth it: heartaches, backaches and all," more than likely we are handling the true tasks of our existence.

When we feel that our acts count in our own eyes, when these mean something to us in the overall scheme of existence, we generally are energized. By asking ourselves, "How do I feel now?" after we've accomplished something difficult, we can read our feelings as the text of our life's story. This reading helps us know ourselves.

Here, in the presence of our daily life or practical outcomes, our guidelines are primarily subjective. When faithful to our essential nature and to our dream of what life could be at its best, we usually experience lasting satisfaction even if, in themselves, our activities were unspectacular.

POSITIVE STRUCTURING FOR FINDING INTRINSIC PURPOSE—A SAMPLE EXERCISE

Phase I: Exploration—Discovering "What"

Positive Structuring can help us reawaken lost, unexpressed or latent personal vision.* A reasonable opening step in finding our intrinsic purposes is to use the dictionary to explore the definitions and our own understanding of words such as *vision, dreams, purpose, intention, passion, vocation, calling.* Jung's comment that vocation means our particular calling to be fully human in a specific way and through distinctive acts, choices, and life's work provides an appropriate set of contextual questions at this initial stage.

- How do I sense myself called into being as a "best self"? What does the phrase *best self* mean to me? Would it mean being or doing less, or more, of what I'm currently being or doing?
- What does being my "best self" imply in terms of behavior, my values, work, life outcomes or relationships? Do my present habits or choices help or hinder me?
- What life-purposes must I fulfill in order to experience commitment, creative passion, or feel as if I have found my right vocation? Are there cycles that are peculiarly mine?
- When, for instance, do I feel most involved and alive? Are these productive or self-defeating times? When might I have abandoned

*One caveat: Some people lack vision, wonder why they're getting up in the morning and may have so successfully snuffed out their basic instinct for vigorous life expression that they require therapy. In cases of consistent joylessness, self-sabotage or serious emotional disorders, Positive Structuring is only a helpful adjunct to professional, clinical help. We must remember that Positive Structuring evolved as my way of helping healthy, dynamically active business people create solutions—not as a clinical technique to treat depression, deep resentment or suicidal impulses.

myself—and supported myself—and what have these acts contributed to my life today?

- In what ways does who I am contribute to my family, community or country? If I were better-educated (wealthier, younger, older, etc.), what more would I be doing in my talent, value or goal area? What must I do to move in that direction anyway?

Phase II: Research—Plumbing the Depths

Next, we try to bring a useful context to all of this. In some way, our answers to Phase I's inquiries will begin to point us to the spirit of our life's destiny. We may want to observe people whom we sense embody the productive, inspiring purposes that we seek. It is critical that we not merely list people whom others tell us are inspiring. For instance:

- Who charms or attracts me? Why? How do I interpret this?
- What does my admiration of such people tell me—what does the appeal of their actions, their life-intent, reveal to me? Might I be suppressing some quality they express?
- What do I feel or notice in their way of being, values, contributions, life, their words, voices, bodies or facial expressions? How and why do these remind me of positive elements or drives in myself?
- Can I locate directional tendencies or deeper lessons in this psychic attraction? Are there latent talents or drives in me that those whom I admire stimulate?
- What values or responsibilities do my chosen role models have that I may want to adopt?
- What do my answers tell me about the life that I currently live? What do my answers say about the future I want most?
- If I can identify a consistent set of values, actions, responsibilities, etc., how might I gain deeper understanding of my own spiritual requirements?

Such questions can surface authentic answers during both daily activities and in our dreams at night. A competent analyst or spiritual director (especially someone well versed in Jungian or Transpersonal methods of psychology) can be a tremendous ally during these early phases of exploration. Asking ourselves open-ended questions—say, before sleep—can stimulate vivid dreams for which interpretive help is needed. In time, we can expand into more advanced tasks of Positive Structuring.

Phase III: Solution Architecture—Creating Models

Our next objective is to travel beyond verbal or intellectual understanding into a construction of viable activities for ourselves—activities that we consciously link to our vision or goals. What I call architectural study models need not be three-dimensional, but they should ideally inform, inspire, motivate and energize us. We might create a unique notebook or "nonlinear" list of meaningful life-purposes. For instance, during this phase one man collected a library of audiotaped and videotaped interviews that especially appealed to him and that dealt with the issues of his own vision. For months he simply recorded radio and television interviews. Then he reviewed his tape library to dig out information about his own life to find out what else he needed to do. He first moved along the lines of the questions listed above and only after that began collecting tapes. His tape collection was his resource. To his glad surprise, he discovered that all his tapes involved arduous, high achievement. He saw that although he had designed his life to be secure and comfortable (having listened to family and friends who told him to "take it easy"), his true joy and life's ambition was to accomplish something far beyond his normal comfort level. In this same way, others have used music, photographic composites, or short stories as their earliest Phase III tasks. The object is to locate the *patterns* inherent in their earlier research notes, self-observances and revelations.

Lengthier Phase III Positive Structuring Tasks: Basking in the Fine Arts

We might make a three- or four-month study of the finest art, music or sculpture available to us. For this we can visit galleries or museums or scrutinize books with high-quality photographs on painting, tapestry, sculpture or architecture.* We can learn to scan quickly, then

---

*Or any art form that we prefer and naturally are drawn to.

return to study more thoroughly, those works that have caught our eye. We look for whatever touches us—our values and deepest interior drives soon become obvious. We may notice that we are especially moved by works about animals, nature, food, children, the downtrodden or superheroes. This data holds a key to, or a message about, our life's vision. Someone who finds she is made happy by words, letters and type might then investigate hobbies or vocational outlets like typography, calligraphy and other forms of lettered printmaking. Someone else who is lifted up by music, by weaving or by any other art forms will soon spot other clues about his larger purposes.

Once we have saturated our consciousness with the images and language of art or music, we may become aware of repeating ideas or elements, or discover that our interest is sparked by a dominant theme or motif—a predictable stimulus or means of activation. Perhaps these profoundly move, motivate or upset us. If we can talk over our discoveries with a trusted, hopefully gifted, friend or counselor, we can enlist collegial help in the fascinating interpretive process that ensues. Our object is to study our choices and patterns of response, and to locate emotional and behavioral clues about that which we seek—in this case, a life worth living, some heightened individual passion or purpose.

Since all fine art directs us to the hidden mysteries of our psyche, Positive Structuring frequently relies on the fine arts. This is not to say that everyone must become an artist, but that truly superior art encodes humanity's universal values, strivings and most poignant frustrations. In these elements, we often find ourselves and our life's path.

The study of painting, music, literature, Scriptures, poetry, theater and dance awakens subterranean levels of clustered insights and connects discontinuous bits of experience wherein one idea leads to another. Soon we remember or understand what we feel, fear or yearn for. The purity, subtlety and intensity of our feeling life is restored as we reunite with universal messages of hope, despair, beauty or adventure. This world of images, sounds and movement provides constant, steady commentary about human joy and struggle, guides us through a solitary observational pilgrimage to our deepest heart, our own truths and aspirations. "When I was getting divorced," one man said, "I felt so defeated—the props, all the meaning, had been knocked out of my life. Walking through my local museum one day, I saw a huge, wall-sized quilt with strange, sophisticated and humorous creatures in every square. The deep, sad humor buoyed me up—made me remember that better times lay ahead and gave me the stimulus to express something intelligent from within, as the artist had done."

CASE STUDY: ANOTHER PROFILE OF MASTERY

The theater holds marvelous Positive Structuring potential. By simply
attending plays, ballets or concerts (or then advancing to act or dance
in a class or a neighborhood theater), we stimulate buried emotions,
language and bodily sensibilities that we may have denied or long
forgotten.* One man I will call Tom† realized that he undermined
himself with apathy and lack of energy. After getting into the spirit of
the traits and attitudes of what he thought was his vision, Tom under-
went a series of deep tissue massages called Rolfing. He also enrolled
in a modern dance class. His initial goal was simply to reawaken his
vitality, find his enthusiasm and drive. After a few months, Tom pro-
gressed to the more rigorous study of a classical martial art. Within a
year, he felt and looked like a wholly new person. His body—muscle
tone and movements, his posture—an increased resonance in his voice,
his lively expression, all spoke of a revived and regenerated man. Tom's
energy, drive and vision had been on hold, held in his musculature. As
he restored his inmost self, his outer life became vibrant as well. Tom's
original plan had been to understand why he was so blocked. Positive
Structuring showed him "why," and also gave him a way out: first
through bodywork, then through a tangible study model, his real life
began to unfold.

Tom realized that he had thoroughly thwarted his best impulses. He
impeded everything he tried to do. He now found that his single
current ambition was to write polished and precise short stories that
might endure. Over time, subsequent Positive Structuring projects
began to address this dream. He designed an architectural project that
spanned several months: the creation of one room in his house that
epitomized the type of short story he wanted to write: sparse and clear.
Later Tom remarked that his multistaged construction project taught
him about other significant traits he needed if he was to become a
decent writer. For instance, he knew that without his family's cooperation and support the room—and his stories—would never be completed. Ordinarily, the old Tom would have suppressed his wishes and

---

*Again: a public acting class is not a place to work out our traumas and resentments.
Positive Structuring is a technique for psychologically healthy, spiritually evolving
people who want to grow in 21st-century thinking and creative adaptive skill. Those
who have serious emotional problems should find psychologists who use psychodrama
techniques.
†Tom is another composite of many individuals who report a similar line of self-help
success.

then been incredibly fatigued as a result—all his creative drive trapped and turned against himself. The new Tom quietly asserted himself. "I'm proud of myself," he reported. "With dignity, I let my wife and sons know that I need time alone, that I must have privacy and a separate space in which to work. To my amazement, they said, 'Fine.' It was only a big deal to me."

Not surprisingly, Tom constructed a one-room writing studio. Eventually, he included in it all the design subtleties of light, color and state-of-the-art office equipment that he required in order to take himself seriously as a writer. Whereas previously Tom discounted his needs (and therefore denied himself energy and opportunity to do what he did best), he now told himself and others the truth:

> Creating this room was my assertion on many levels. The room became a metaphor and a concrete evidence of my own existence. Moreover, through the room's construction process, I gained insight into what I need for energy, enthusiasm and self-esteem. My writing now holds a place of honor in my life, and in a real way I—the core of me—exist as never before.

Like Tom, we can create models that lead us to our vision. We can also use anything we're doing to notice what's meaningful, here and now. With a clear mind, it is relatively easy to move backward: from present involvements to our current, if hidden, truths. We don't mechanistically follow these phases in an unimaginative, lockstep or rigid manner. We simply look, with discernment, on how we do all things, employing our normal actions and choices as metaphors (or as a mirror) of our motives and directions. When a friend built her own home, she realized she was constructing it without conventional walls:

> I wanted to move the walls, to change the interior, on a whim rather than boxing myself into one fixed living arrangement. I saw that in my life, work and relationships, I also wanted the flexibility to change, move around and be free to follow the impulses of the moment.

If we pay attention to what exists, neutrally accepting our observations, we can use the substrata of daily life to read our purposes. Positive

Structuring is not a method for endlessly striving after idealized, but largely empty, ambitions. It is true: The technique does encourage achievement. This is because it accelerates activity and the physical demonstrations of what we want. But raising awareness—not accomplishment—is its primary goal. Sometimes life-purposes can also be found just by looking at what exists and embracing that.

I believe list-making and conventional, too linear goal-setting exercises are, by now, outdated.* These provide just a pale outline of what we are interiorly and do little to illuminate our thought processes. On the other hand, when we apply ourselves incrementally and with imagination to constructing distinctive physical or experiential representations of our values and goals, we begin to believe in—and build up—their attainability. We are systematically externalizing our positive forward movement or thoughts. We also instruct ourselves in the subtleties of each goal's requirements. This helps us become responsible to those things we say we want. With Positive Structuring, the dictionary, pictures, fine art, music, the theater, architecture, even other people lead us to the images surrounding our life's journey. Then heightened intuition and discernment further reveal the organic theme behind these. Instead of merely asking for advice or taking antiseptic inventory of our long-range goals, Positive Structuring invites us to look into our minds, connect with and then trust the richness of our own thinking. When we can truthfully acknowledge our good sense and natural lucidity, multiple intelligences reveal themselves. These usually hidden gifts display our true colors. Once seen in this manner, no matter how ordinary on the surface, our vision is extraordinary. Ultimately, by concretely structuring our values, goals and vision into conscious awareness, we demonstrate ourselves—which is to say we allow our mind and heart to be known.

---

*Alexander Stoddard's book *Living a Beautiful Life,* my own *Elegant Choices, Healing Choices,* Moshe Feldenkrais's *The Elusive Obvious* or Charles D. Hayes's *Self-University* are four very dissimilar works that, nevertheless, outline numerous specific ways to increase self-awareness. Whether through aesthetics, choice-making, values, movement or education, we can *build* metaphors to identify our life's highest goals. All it takes is keen desire to grow and learn. As Charles Hayes writes, your desire to learn is the tuition price you must pay for your answers.

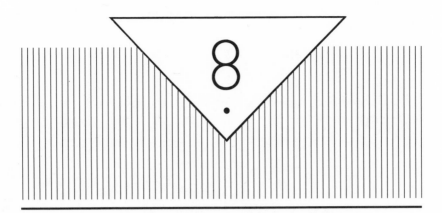

A 21st-CENTURY MIND TRANSCENDS OR RESOLVES PARADOX

let all go—the
big small middling
tall bigger really
the biggest and all
things—let all go
dear
   so comes love

E. E. CUMMINGS

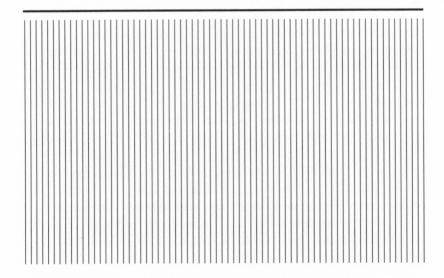

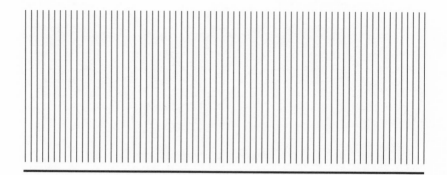

Some months ago I presented a seminar for a high-powered women's group. All were wives of major corporation presidents, accomplished and articulate in their own right. Yet even among these bright, achieving women, I sensed variations in problem-solving and creative adaptive skill. For example, some managed their time effectively, and were well able to accommodate their own needs and interests in what was an impressively overloaded calendar of events. Others were overwhelmed by activities that their husband's position imposed on them. The successful time managers also took better care of their own physical and spiritual requirements—attended classes or church, carved out quiet times during each day when they could rest, meditate or simply be. Those who complained about lack of time were unable to pull away. They freely admitted feeling torn between their marital responsibilities and their very human desire to grow as individuals. This group believed themselves stuck and could not transcend their life's opposing pulls. Indeed, they were hemmed into restrictive, stereotypical Superwoman roles—more by perception than by circumstance.

Our own tendency to dutifully accept or give in to what, on the surface, seems to be a prisonlike situation often is the result of our own underdevelopment. We have probably all felt unable to solve a problem and have lived with our dilemma, perhaps for a few years. Then one day, "suddenly", we see our way clear of the matter. It seems not so much that time heals our fragmented overview of the problem, but that with time we have a chance to sort out the variables involved. We play with diverse combinations or solutions, experiment with different ways of reconciling the matter. As we relinquish old, unproductive thoughts, or rise to a higher plane of awareness, new answers come.

Emotion, entrenchment, fear and confusion all hinder problem solving. As we mature into a problem, become familiar with its special dimensions or character, our self-awareness develops as well. Gradually, we bring our best—most objective and creative—thinking into play. Something in ourselves, as well as in the circumstance, corrects. The skill of resolving paradox seems built upon three key perceptual traits:

- the ability to reconcile discordant elements or see things as "non-dual."
- the ability to "detach" emotionally, or let go, to remove ourselves and bring a nonentrenched mind to the issue.
- the ability to think and even behave in metaphorical terms.

Each of these—and more—is an aspect of a unitive mind that accompanies our growth of awareness. The implications of having such skills are vast, given that the 21st century promises to be a time of enormous cultural diversity. Multiple languages, values and expectations already proliferate in almost every city and workplace. Not long ago, while visiting British Columbia, I stayed at a popular top-ranking hotel. Tourist brochures, menus and every other piece of hotel literature was written in several languages. Asian languages preceded English. Soon after, in Los Angeles, I noticed how many ethnic "villages" had supplanted L.A.'s typical ambience. One entire thoroughfare is now a small Vietnamese town, complete with artifacts, hanging calligraphic banners, restaurants, shops and churches. For several miles, it is as if one were in Asia, since all this reflected the tastes and culture of these newcomers. A few miles away was an authentic Middle Eastern community, and around another bend lay a Spanish sector. If anyone feels that the 1980s brought confusion or conflicts because of altered values and roles of men, women or sociopolitical groups, it is safe to say that this trend will accelerate. If there ever was an era in which to learn how to resolve conflict or harmonize divergent interests, this seems it.

PULLING TOGETHER DISCORDANT ELEMENTS

Almost everyone feels stymied on occasion. Some remind themselves that if they just let matters be, "sleep on it," things will work themselves out. One man ascribed his job unhappiness to money—or lack of it. However, he believed he could find his way clear of the problem.

I want to be a counselor more than anything, and I know I'm talented along these lines. I have tremendous desire to give of myself, and enough credits to get my credentials. Lack of money is my problem. It costs money to rent office space, and build a practice. I know in a year or so I'll figure out a way, win the lottery or take on another job. But right now I don't know which way to go on this.

In contrast, a woman told me she blames her parents and early training for the out-of-reach quality of her "true calling." While the man I've quoted knows that he will eventually find his way, this woman's mind seems confined, has a narrower focus and is unable to transcend its anxious, authority-pleasing focus:

Ever since I was small, I've known I was supposed to do something creative, but was discouraged along these lines. I was forced to be "responsible," to meet the requirements my parents and society set for me. I have tried to break these barriers that block my finest self-expressions, but now can't remember what I wanted to do—I knew what my vocation was in the past, but now feel clouded, can't recall what it was that captivated me. With each day, I grow more anxious. I'm enraged at my parents for having raised me the way they did.

Her tendency to polarize, judge harshly and pessimistically, her mind's solidly unyielding cause-and-effect construction are apparent.

All truly creative adaptive minds somehow suspend judgments, resolve dichotomies, fuse conflicting elements. This is not to imply that such persons are superhuman or never blame or feel polarized. But their minds possess an open awareness—are acutely sentient and alert. Even if problems remain unsolved, the individual lives harmoniously with his or her asymmetries, knowing that solutions will come in time. For instance, people who feel they have the talent to make a go of a particular profession, yet who—like the man quoted above—lack funds for an office or office staff, sometimes wait patiently for years, planning all the while around their obstacles. Then they might start the business at home, or perhaps they have the self-confidence to borrow enough start-up funds. They transcend the "no money" versus "I yearn to do this" contradiction, if only bit by bit. Those creative adaptives who believe they have not addressed their personal needs because of family or society's expectations don't get caught up in assessing blame. Often they turn to books or therapy for assistance. Or they insert themselves into a sphere of influence of helpful, supportive friends or find mentors who nurture their emerging growth. Rather than castigating others or thinking along all-is-lost lines, they chip away at their problem until it loses density and power. In varying ways and means, they somehow settle the "me" versus "others" conflict peacefully, even if their process takes time. As a final example, I have met ethical people in business who can work in companies that sometimes seem to require a compromise of ethics. They manage this without undue guilt or polarization of either individuals or issues. They are not seduced into personal dishonesty or denial of what's really going on. Rather, they use themselves (and their value systems) as correctives, to help improve the tone of their company's or colleagues' decision making. Somehow this involves rising above problems and functions perceptually in ways that serve their own and others' good. I am not suggesting that we "bliss out" or suspend discernment and judgment in everyday life. This is not a way to judge whether, say, the baby-sitter is competent or not. I am advocating we use this excellent tool of intellect when we want to resolve paradox.

EMBRACING PARADOX

If we consider our own past insights and discoveries, we could find we already have transcended what once seemed to us impossibly discordant pulls. This memory shows us how we embrace paradox. We need not be philosophers or enlightened gurus to resolve life's contradictions. Almost everyone has experience with resolutions such as these:

- Something in our business or creative life actually expands or profits as we cut back, prune and limit our efforts.
- We are rewarded or receive more as we let go or relax our efforts than when striving to get, exploit or force an issue,
- We prosper enormously when profiting others and when forgetting about our own interests.
- Over time, enormous benefits come to us (and to others) from what we felt at first was a "selfish" act.

- Lasting lessons or some true good accrues from the very problem or outcome we initially fear or find most painful.
- Small "deaths" or soul-wrenching relinquishings open us up to a larger, fuller or richer life.
- Out of failures, mistakes or unhappy events, we find opportunities for growth or find or create precepts that we then productively apply to other realms of our life.

All these examples illustrate the way in which a developing mind aligns itself and becomes easy with what, at first, it perceived as conflict, discord or threat. As a friend reported:

I learned over the course of my life that we live in a upside-down world. Everything I was taught was one way actually turns out to be quite another. I wish I had known this when I was a youngster.

Like Alice who fell down the rabbit hole, we, too, may wonder where all of this activity will take us or where we are going to come out. Neither Alice nor we should worry. The unitive influence on a mind that penetrates its center produces release, wakefulness, harmony and love. Moreover, such a mind becomes creatively intelligent. Sometimes, just "sleeping on" a problem allows us to come into contact with our higher faculties and thus solve a problem.

Undeniably, each of us touches different levels of awareness, brings varying degrees of consciousness to our daily concerns or conflicts. For instance, almost all of the women in my workshop wanted to pursue their own formal education, yet only a handful managed to accomplish this, given their other responsibilities. These few had returned to college to earn advanced degrees. Others addressed their need for intellectual stimulation by joining book-club discussions. One or two regularly attended evening lectures, museums or weekend workshops.

Only those women who felt they couldn't reserve any time for themselves were unable to maneuver through their clashing needs. They sounded much like people who give "excellent reasons" for remaining imprisoned in a job they hate. They want to leave, but talk themselves out of their feelings by continually listing their rationale for staying. One woman believed she slighted her husband's needs when she attended night school. He told her he felt deprived when she was away, and couldn't perform his job properly when she was unavailable as his dinner partner during nights out with clients and staff. She knew that to further her education she would have to save some evenings for herself, but interpreted her need as "selfish."

> I'm indecisive about this. I want to be there for my husband. I also want to study music at a graduate level. But I'm trapped in others' definitions of what I should and should not do. I don't want to be a people-pleaser, yet in a way I do. I feel I'm reversing some original agreement that my husband and I had about my role, which was to be at his side as a supporter.

Another woman faced and mastered the same issue, reconciling the seeming contradiction between her thirst for knowledge and her role as a faithful sidekick, wife and hostess:

> I don't view myself as "selfish" when I do something for myself that, ultimately, benefits my husband or our family. I look at things through the long view. Even if something appears selfish, at a deeper level it isn't.
>
> When I returned for my master's degree, I saw immediately that the more I grew into a full, well-rounded person, the more I contributed to others, both at home and in my role as a VIP's wife. Now I hold my own in a conversation. I have my own point of view. Sure it was inconvenient to us all, but it was worth it. In the long run, there was nothing selfish about my choice.

Another woman described having watched her own mother give "selflessly" to her children in martyrlike fashion. This giving eventually produced guilt and unhappiness on everyone's part and couldn't be called a solution, since this choice put the family in turmoil.

No uniform thought-language resolves all paradox. In creative adaptives' thinking, a pattern is noticeable within the sphere of conflict resolution: Those who resolve discord accept what is, at least to some degree. They embrace reality as it exists here and now, neatly blending both passive and active attitudes in their thinking and behavior.

The more vocal among the corporate wives were those who embraced their traditional wifely roles, yet also took care of their personal development needs. They said that they asserted themselves fully when they first sensed a conflict. I suspect that as able, vigorous communicators, they quickly and firmly encouraged their spouses to pay attention, lend support and take them seriously. This is what I mean by "active." On the other hand, they also sustained their previously agreed-upon marital obligations, participated enthusiastically and willingly in their husband's corporate events. They entertained when necessary, dressed their part, were present when needed most, and so on. Instead of resisting this dimension of commitment, their acquiescence—or enjoyment of their role—must somehow influence outcomes in their favor.

This mix of active/passive postures is a subtle, pragmatic affair. It involves synthesizing ideas and opposing beliefs or values deeply in consciousness so that when solutions are found, they are not experienced as severe compromises or as answers that cause everyone to forfeit what they really want.* If a richly felt love is absent in such domestic negotiations, then anger, resentment or feelings of powerlessness dominate. This mood contaminates the smooth outcome of any agreement. Martin Buber once wrote that real love causes us to live in the direction of the other person's experience. Creative adaptives fuse others' needs with the often sharp, opposing edges of their own needs and interests. A softer, reconfigured blend of both parties' needs results.

YOU ARE AN AGENT OF CHANGE: MOVING TOWARD DETACHMENT

At times we all need a jolt to wake us up to our next step or increase our objectivity about our circumstances. This seems especially so when, emotionally, we are heavily invested in a situation. Counselors, spiritual directors, books, support groups, can all be helpful at different times and for different people. In some cases, a crisis shocks us into emotional detachment and provokes our letting go of an entrenched position. At other times, a friend's chance remark may open up our eyes, make us feel, "Thanks, I needed that." Sometimes our own stuckness is painful. We watch ourselves spend months and months, even years, without addressing a problem. Our dilemma, lethargy, bad habit or toxic relationship persists. Caught in the quagmire of our depression or indecision, one day we realize we are boring ourselves. We finally understand

---

*For an excellent methodology along these lines, see Fisher and Ury's *Getting to Yes*, the popular negotiations classic from the Harvard Negotiation Project.

that if things are going to improve, we must be the authors and agents of that change. Then we get busy. Such awakenings are often due more to our having detached emotionally than to any particularly brilliant insight. Again, letting go cultures the love, clarity or energy required to see through dense circumstances.

Certain events can revive us in this way. The birth of a child often triggers a burst of recognition. We see that we have much work to do in the world, if not for ourselves, then for our offspring. We mature quickly, become responsible. A solid marriage, a friend's death, a line of poetry—even a walk along a beach—may suddenly cause self-correction or help us actively address whatever needs attention.

When we truly despair, therapy helps, as it can during our impasses—when we don't know what to do or when we've tried everything and still feel lost. Then, too, if we need huge amounts of time to sort matters out or gain our bearings, we can recall Milton's observation, "They also serve who only stand and wait." Pulling too hard on ourselves to achieve or grow can be counterproductive. It's often helpful to let go of our own efforts, our "push" to become unstuck. I get letters that tell me many, if not most, people need reminders to go slowly, to allow themselves opportunities for rest and regression.

The good news is that often as we let go, we progress faster. People have told me that when they stop trying to find that magic "start" button, when they release themselves from a forced, brutal will-to-succeed in worldly terms, precisely then something within shifts productively. As they relinquish their bid for speedy growth, they see improvements, solve urgent problems—miraculously, their answers come. This is true acceptance. Some call it forgiveness. Whatever our term, as we soften our too-aggressive effort to be other than what we are, we change. At the exact point of our release or self-acceptance, we expand, become more.

This integration of discordant elements is what artists do, and thoroughly enjoy doing, as they solve problems of color or design. They blend conflicting hues or shapes in a way that preserves and accommodates the integrity of each. Part of our interest in a well-painted picture comes from the limits that an artist has experienced, either in terms of the materials used, the size of the work or her own technical limitations. In some form, when an artist works with an awareness of selective constraints, he or she always produces enhanced outcomes, a fresher, more original or more poignant work than when fighting against the medium. The inherent limitation is a given—not a reason to back away from the work.

We can learn to apply the skill of using our flaws and limitations to a wider life canvas. In part our ability to go with what we are comes with emotional maturity. Additionally, a mix of cognitive strengths provides the heightened awareness that lets us use our blemishes creatively. If we do this, we advance, rather than defeat, our life. For instance, when we are intellectually robust, we can examine ourselves honestly, perhaps with a touch of good humor. Eventually, we find a neat fit between what we do well and what we must let others do for us and our own best solution. Not long ago, a good friend heard me struggling with a long-standing family problem and reflected, "It sounds to me as though you know what your limits are." Although usually I do know my limits, in this case I was barely conscious of them until her words put the matter into an easy-to-manage, clarifying context. Later, when talking with my relatives about the issue, I heard myself say, "I won't take on that problem—I know my limits, and this is beyond me." The resolution of this particular matter was so simple, once I had let go of my habitual perspective and gained objectivity. Sometimes a friend or counselor can help us see through our blind spots. This seeing-through dissolves many contradictions and opposing pulls.

Detaching emotionally also alleviates paralyzing fear. When we are relatively open, we think along integrative lines. Nonentrenchment, or our willingness to examine whatever is unattractive, produces a big-picture perspective, helps us see things in their larger contexts and thus reconcile many superficial dichotomies.

METAPHORS RECONCILE CONTRADICTIONS

The ability to think in metaphorical terms is a third skill that resolves paradox. A workshop participant in Boston brought this idea to our group when she described how she corrected her tendency to be a perfectionist:

> I used to see my life as a white sheet: it had to be all clean, perfectly stainless. Then I started noticing that this sheet—my life—was sprinkled with stains where I'd made mistakes or detours. Looking at my life that way was negative. All I saw was spots that I wanted to hide—I thought everyone was supposed to have a "white, blemish-free sheet."

Then it occurred to me to revise my thinking—try to see life not as a white sheet but as a multicolored, brightly patched quilt. Viewed that way, each so-called spot adds to the quilt's richness and variety. Its composition grows more interesting with time, not less. Even the mistakes and personal redirections added to my life. It was a very positive perceptual stance, and made a world of difference in my self-esteem.

While almost everyone understands this metaphor and appreciates its liberating power, it is surprising how few people create their own metaphors. Those who view the world in poetic or metaphorical terms promote their own transcendence over problems. They abandon old, outworn boundaries and fuse an issue's odd or ill-fitting elements so that they see harmoniously. Like poets or other artists, almost everyone has the innate ability to tap insightfully into his or her nonconscious realms.

Some people find it easy to reconcile opposites. They can teach these solutions to others, leading them into novel, fresh perception. For instance, the woman in my Boston workshop elevated the awareness of everyone in the group simply by sharing her quilt metaphor. Without trying, she taught our class how to reinterpret their life's mistakes, setbacks and redirections more positively. I saw their eyes click their new understanding into place. Like Margaret Mead, this creative adaptor "raised common sense to a new level." Because she thought conceptually, then acted in self-liberating directions, those around her benefited. Rather than avoid discomfort, this woman befriended her conflict with creative vision and then showed others how to do the same—taught them to openly approach their disharmonies and see their pain with friendly eyes.

Gifted poets teach us how to think metaphorically. Through their use of words and idea-pictures, poets artfully arrange the familiar and mundane within fresh, new frames. Even a somber poem can playfully, lightly, draw us into meditation that produces insight. If we reflect on it, the poet's heightened awareness becomes a teacher for our own.

The Greek poet Archilochus's line, "The fox knows many things, but the hedgehog knows one big thing," is a case in point. On the surface, the poet is simply describing two animals. But when we ask ourselves why his sentence is so hauntingly truthful, we find a theme within a theme. Instinctively, we understand the hidden message. The words remind us that we are exactly like these small, familiar beasts. Some people are foxes. Quick, sly and crafty, mentally these individuals are always darting about, coming and going in and out of facts, figures or gossip. Whatever their attraction or charm, foxes (and foxlike people) lack the density, strength and power of hedgehog types, immersed in only one large, essential reality. Hedgehogs, the poet says, look beneath the impermanent, ever-changing landscape of externals, relating everything to some deep truth, or wide-angled, eternal vision. This line of poetry unifies our understanding of the world because the poet helps us see through his own, no doubt hedgehog, eyes—draws us away from the fox's distracting mind and brings us into our own whole-sight.

Creative adaptors seem much like hedgehogs to me. They, too, see, or exist in, one broad-based, eternal reality. Like my articulate Boston workshop participant, what they know and strive to communicate deepens our own discoveries. Their insights and solutions stem from some primary intuitive process that allows quite predictable leaps of consciousness by which they transcend paradox. Nor must this necessarily happen on a grand or glamorous scale. Someone who views work as play or who lives responsibly, seriously, while simultaneously retaining strong childlike tendencies, whose life honors heart, humor and intellect, whose self-interest merges so fully with the interests of the other as to be inseparable, demonstrates creative adaptation. Yet we must know such persons well (or look at their lives deeply) to discern any differences between their outward appearance and, say, our own.

DETACHING EMOTIONALLY AND ACTUALLY

When we feel trapped, we can take immediate small steps to extricate ourselves from the blinders we put on. Using the Positive Structuring approach, we might move through the first stages until we become thoroughly familiar with the thing or state of mind we hope to have. This means engrossing ourselves in solutions—not in the problem. Then we design a physical or experiential study model to enter playfully into this new, improved reality.

For instance, I recently conducted a master's workshop for professional therapists and career counselors. Prior to the course, most of them identified several problems they hoped to address. Eighty-five percent of their concerns related to overcommitment and time frustrations. They had trouble balancing family and professional demands. I suggested the group consider pruning as a Positive Structuring model. By this I meant the gardening term, the act of cutting back vegetation. Cropping certain plants fosters more beautiful and luxuriant new growth than would sprout if the plant just ran wild. For example, if hybrid tea roses are not pruned thoroughly every winter, they do not blossom well in late spring. Workshop participants who were gardeners used this idea as a physical study model to help themselves actually put this "law" into practice. Each person who tried this began to notice links between intelligently cutting back one's plants and actually cutting back one's real-world activities. After the workshop exercise, one woman organized a neighborhood car pool to save time chauffeuring her children. A health care manager reviewed his workload and realized he could delegate more to other staff members. This was his real-world "pruning." These quite obvious solutions somehow didn't occur to them before. The power of the cropping metaphor (and, in some cases, the experience of pruning plants) allowed group members to enter an authentic, low-risk circumstance from which practical life-solutions emerged. The hands-on, metaphorical activity somehow stimulates a new—or latent—neurological "memory" from which next steps evolve.

As noted, if we just reflect on a few select lines of poetry, mull these over as we go about our day or while sitting quietly undisturbed, we accomplish a great deal. The poet's paradigm becomes ours. Suppose we are worrying about how to let go of something—or someone. This E. E. Cummings poem can help us enter the spirit of relinquishment:

> let it go—the
> smashed word broken
> open vow or
> oath cracked length
> wise—let it go it
> was sworn to
>
> go
>
> . . . let it go—the
> truthful liars and
> the false fair friends
> and the boths and
> neithers—you must let them go they
> were born
>
> to go. (P. 96)

If we step into Cummings's awareness—even for just an instant—we may elevate our own. In itself, this method of thinking through a superb poet's empathic thought process offers consolation for the pain we feel when facing the continual necessity of relinquishment. As with all fine art, sensitive poetry cultivates an elevated mind, especially when the poet has experienced what we ourselves are feeling.

SOME SAMPLE PHASE III STUDY MODELS TO HELP US "LET GO"

Perhaps our inability to let go is linked to our habitual tendencies to cling in daily life. A concrete Positive Structuring model that teaches us about letting go can be either experiential or physical. Throwing things out (or giving them away to charities) is a useful practical exercise. Metaphysician and writer Catherine Ponder once wrote that if we want prosperity (or even specific new possessions), we should start toward our goals by discarding all the saved, stored or never-used items in our closet, garage or files. She taught that when people create a vacuum, they help nature rush in to fill it with those things they are dreaming about.

One woman invented this study model in order to practice relinquishment:

> I taught myself to release overattachment by giving away items I valued. Nothing excessive, you understand, just things I felt still had use or were pretty. I gave my garden's prize flowers to friends when visiting. I made gifts of books, clothes and canned goods that were perfectly suited to me. Some things I just donated.
>
> The point? To teach myself that my happiness isn't in things, that I can survive material loss and that I, as a human being, am larger than my lusts and fears. I'm glad to say I have experienced much benefit. I feel freer, know myself as generous. The critical thing is that now I'm also giving up my old—if still attractive—emotional baggage. There is a connection between mind and matter.

When we sense ourselves to be in a spiritual crisis or know ourselves to be one way but dearly want to change, we may not feel we have the strength to relinquish our emotional or other "baggage." Even here the physical model just described can help. Eventually, our actions bring relief. But first—perhaps for a long time—we work with what we have, do whatever it is that we can do to take ourselves along the route we want.

ACCEPTING THE PAIN OF LETTING GO

One reader described his keen reluctance to go forward with a life he knew he needed. Whenever he considered remedying his long-standing mistaken ways, fear of painful consequences conflicted with his desire to change.

Daily I struggle with one question: How do I get "out" of a past decision that I know is wrong in such a way that I don't hurt myself? I know we aren't meant to suffer forever for our mistakes, but find myself unable to extricate myself from something that is a grave error. Must I "pay" with negative experiences in order to drop old patterns? Mostly I'm afraid I can't yet see a way to go.

Perhaps one part of letting go, or getting unstuck, is the willingness to undergo pain. Could this be a key to our advancement as persons? Such pain has its own rhythm. There is no question that growing up as a human being involves relinquishment. We might sacrifice living unconsciously. We might cease worrying about someone's opinion of us, or give up some material benefit, like a promotion, in order to develop as persons. We can easily outgrow certain superior attitudes.

I've met people who stay in unproductive, low-paying jobs because they believe their job has greater value or dignity than a glamorous, high-paying job. This reverse elitism makes such individuals feel that poverty is, in itself, better than affluence, that all wealthy people are superficial or sinful, or that they sully their hands by climbing the corporate ladder. In a way, they remove themselves, drop out of, a fully participative life. For them, making a sacrifice may mean joining the stream of life, learning to cooperate with others, dropping their "superior" stance or accepting their place—whatever it naturally is—in the general scheme of interactive affairs.

In addition to avoiding pain, most people also hate to hurt others. This is yet another cause of hanging on to problems. Sometimes our growth pains others who don't want us to leave or "graduate" into our own lives. When people aren't properly managing their lives, for instance, they often resist our growth. When our desire for the good outweighs our desire for comfort, approval or old patterns of security, then we become willing to accept life's pains—even can resolve this matter of hurting others.

Once, a woman in one of my audiences said she thought everyone involved in change or personal growth should have grief counseling. Apparently, she reconciled hurting others by likening the experience to a small death, an organic part of her life.

People may leave friends and family as their maturity level surpasses these persons'. Someone's financial success may reveal to her that former habits are unproductive. She may leave the life-style of family, community or peer group. As the consciousness of such people expands, it becomes impossible for them to remain in the neat grooves of their past. So it is not merely that we hurt ourselves—as in the pain of homesickness—when we leave the family nest, but that we know, perhaps unconsciously, that whatever we do differently intrudes on someone else's expectations and comfort.

It is often easier for us to hurt ourselves than to hurt others. This may be especially true for people who know they're in dysfunctional relationships. Even admitting the truth about our experience and feelings can and will hurt. Personal psychological growth doesn't mean we have to leave relationships, but it might mean that. For example, spiritual growth almost always causes separation. A friend reminded me recently of a biblical injunction about this: Scripture warns that we cannot grow into God unless we leave our mother and father. In classical Greek, the feeling behind such departure is called "*miso*," which means hate—a *strong* emotional recoil if others block our way to the Kingdom.

Letting go, whether intellectual or emotional, seems to demand a sort of cooperation, as Saint Bernard wrote, between our free choice and God's grace. Both of these are necessary. There comes that moment when we feel our own internal permission, an opening, to see clearly beyond confusion and obstructions. Only then can we proceed, do what we want, act out our highest intentions. This invitation seems to me a grace. On the other hand, we have to *choose* in this direction, must voluntarily consent to go along with this higher program. This free choice usually involves some element of sacrifice, although it differs from individual to individual.

If, through safe, small, tangible steps, we can court disharmony, say yes to life, move toward discord or resolve contradictions, we grow reconciled to whatever other relinquishments life necessitates. So comes love.

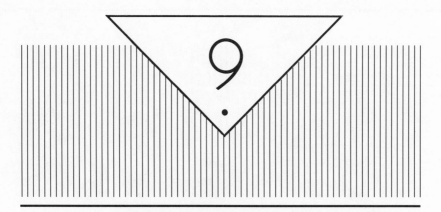

A 21st-CENTURY MIND IS WHOLE-SEEING

The Tao unifies the parts. . . . The sage
rests in the solution of things, and is
dissatisfied with what is not a solution.

LAO-TZU

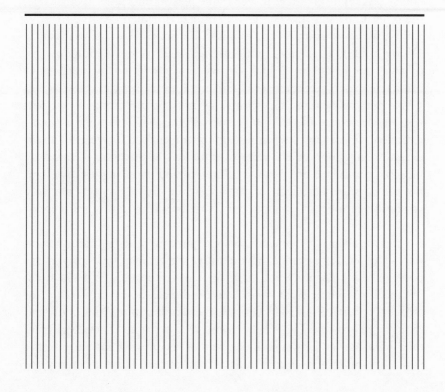

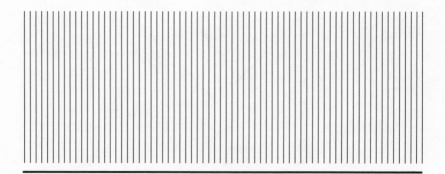

There's an old story about a little boy who finds his room full of horse manure and delightedly cries out, "Oh, good! There's a pony around here somewhere." This tale is generally used to help us turn our minds toward productive ways of thinking by shifting the way we look at things.

Many of us, on finding a room full of manure or any other problematic thing, are crushed or bitter. We perceive this in the worst possible light, believe ourselves unlucky or feel put-upon by fate. Of course, everyone is different. What one person interprets as challenge, the other knows as misery. As we evaluate our own creative adaptive ability, we must examine and monitor our personal, existential stance: Do we hold on to happy or painful memories? Are we going toward, or away from, our own life? Do we say yes or no to fulfilling or profitable experience? Are we embracing lessons that can grow us into whole persons or those that ultimately narrow and diminish our self-respect, autonomy and learning resourcefulness? There is, for example, a massive difference between remaining entrenched for years in a self-defeating addiction or choosing to grow out of this state. Either way means we will face problems. The way of addiction suggests we have not solved some core issue of our life, while growth reflects not only resolution of a central trauma but also a breakthrough in self-expression.

Creative adaptivity depends, in part, on our belief in finding solutions. Do we, for instance, have positive expectancy that answers are possible? At a deeper level, such positive expectancy is based upon instances of whole-sight—our transcendence, however fleeting, of what the poet Rumi called fictions: the world's unrealities, idols and thought structures. Those who manage to separate themselves from their own past and from society's way of seeing gain insight into the neutrality of things, events and circumstances. This objectivity, or clarified awareness, produces the dynamic insight that begins a move toward whole-seeing, personal "final" integration or self-actualization. Whatever name we call it, one of the hallmarks of this development is an overflowing, steady experience of joy.

There are many ways to understand ourselves, to assess why we perceive, or focus on, life as we do. Certainly, variables in categories or types of people have been described in literature as well as in philosophy and psychology.

Positive and negative energies affect self-esteem, worldview, relationships and productivity. In describing nonproductive types, Erich Fromm suggests that it is possible to discern degrees of negativity in such people. They can be just mildly unhappy or, at the other extreme, can exist in a living hell where drive, interests and mood destroy them and all they touch. A rigidly negative self-view makes people deny their need to change or grow. They treat and see themselves as objects, dis"own" their feelings. It is one thing to accept our dark side, quite another to wallow in it or to reject our light.

Our experience surely shows that when we stay too long unhappy, tense or grieving, we greatly diminish overall problem-solving competency. A friend of mine in the throes of a divorce admitted, in her first stages of separation, that she was incapable of putting her mind to any of the huge number of decisions facing her. Widows and widowers know full well how feelings of anger or despair intrude on their readjustment process. These are natural, situational bouts with negativity do not limit creative adaption. Any habitual disposition to despair does. If we are dogged by consistent unhappiness, our entire perceptual system may need overhauling. This, then, is our indicator that a thorough physical workup by a doctor and intensive therapy are in order.

Even extraordinarily creative people, when depressed, find their productivity, self-expression and health undermined. Whatever they produce while under this influence may bear a morose imprint, however veiled. For each of the remarkable few who manage to succeed in life despite depression, there are countless others who simply waste their lives in suffering. Our prisons, urban streets, rehabilitation centers and physicians' offices are filled with case examples.

CREATIVELY SURVIVING CHILDHOOD TRAUMA

Letters that I get from readers who overcame abusive childhoods, conversations with clients who were victimized in early life and research
all indicate that numerous adults do healthfully surmount childhood
trauma. Within the context of an abusive relationship or extremes in
poverty, homelessness or illness, about 15 percent manage to cultivate
exemplary characteristics and skills. In a mysterious fashion, we can
credit this, too, to a grace of sorts, as well as to the primary skills cluster
of the creative adaptive response: These children, often called invulner-
ables by psychologists, *drive toward autonomy, positive self-valuation
and learning resourcefulness.* As youngsters, these individuals shrewdly,
if sometimes unconsciously, protect themselves from environmental or
parental abuses. In so doing, they develop attributes that support them
later, throughout their lives. Research credits their survival, at least in
part, to positive links that they make to healthy adults. (Pines, 1980)
This fact reinforces the inescapable conclusion that positive forces—
like role models or nurturing relationships—are essential for lasting
inner strength and effective outer solutions. Anyone, even in adulthood, can selectively screen in positive memories—or construct them—
if these are lacking. My sense is that this is exactly what invulnerable
children do to survive. We can do the same, if we learn how.

Each of us attends to and interprets our childhood uniquely. We
filter our experiences through different recollective and perceptual
screens. There are as many screens as there are people. From birth (or
before), no two children are alike—even when family conditions and
environment are virtually identical. One child is deeply sensual or
acutely sensitive, the other is tough-skinned and coarse. Birth order,
appearance, physiology or innate temperament, special talents, robust
or weak health, environment and parental treatment are all factors that
influence self-feelings and people's future well-being. For example, the
psychoanalyst Alfred Adler's theory of the importance of birth order
and family positioning to self-esteem and general psychic health may
have flowed more from his own early frailty and helplessness than from
"facts." Adler was a sickly child, unable to compete with his older
brothers or schoolmates. He strongly resented his mother and brothers.
His life's work and his own psychic health can be understood by
studying his memories. By contrast, Eudora Welty's rich, positive re-
membrance of her own childhood reveals another side of this coin.
From Welty's very first lines in *One Writer's Beginnings,* she reveals a

warm, generous memory bank; this may have lent her life its consistent, highly creative drive and its comfort:

> When I was young enough to still spend a long time buttoning my shoes in the morning, I'd listen toward the hall: Daddy upstairs was shaving in the bathroom and Mother downstairs was frying the bacon. They would begin whistling back and forth to each other and down the stairwell. My father would whistle his phrase, my mother would try to whistle, then hum hers back. It was their duet . . . their song almost floated with laughter . . . They kept it running between them, up and down the stairs where I was now just about ready to run clattering down and show them my shoes. (Intro. pages)

Who can say if Welty's childhood actually happened exactly the way she writes of it? Perhaps loving, happy scenes like hers are what she consciously remembers. And who can say how Adler's theories would have changed if he had chosen to attend to other sets of emotions or images from his past? No matter what our own history, we can recast it by the way we hold it in our mind.*

Maharishi Mahesh Yogi's precept, "Whatever you put your attention on grows stronger in your life," neatly describes this phenomenon.

DETERMINING YOUR OWN TYPE: WHO TAUGHT YOU HOW AND WHAT TO THINK?

We need not look to extreme examples to discern how optimism, belief in what is good and possible, helps each of us find solutions and live satisfying lives. Most of us detest being classified into types like objects, but we don't need to fit into a niche in order to survey our basic response mechanisms. For example, we can ask ourselves several open-ended questions to determine the dominant way in which we attend to trouble—and to life in general:

- *Am I generally optimistic or pessimistic?* This catchall question can help us determine the energy we give to problems or with which we

---

*For an extensive discussion on how we do this, see my book *Living Happily Ever After*.

actively move toward solutions. Our answers can show us whether we withdraw from problems when they come up or engage ourselves robustly with solution-finding. I should note that by "pessimism" I do not mean simply expecting the worst, but rather behaving from a deeper, all-pervading gloom to which we surrender. This surrender results in apathy, depression and hopelessness and ultimately drives others away.*

- *How do I react when I feel low or particularly vulnerable?* The healthiest people, emotionally, allow themselves to feel what they feel. Optimism and a productive outlook does not mean a person denies his or her truths or dark days. Quite the reverse: If one can give in to fatigue or sorrow at times, grieve or take vacations or just rest now and then, if one can retreat, talk to a trusted friend, one is emotionally healthier than if he or she stubbornly clings to a rigid picture of cheerfulness or a strict schedule of achievement. When rest is required, when we need to turn to others, to forge stoically ahead seems unnatural and counterproductive.

- *Do I basically like other people?* It is one thing to like other people and choose to be alone (as do many reflective individuals and creative types), and quite another to isolate ourselves because we dislike or distrust people. Some individuals are practically hermits, yet still radiate warmth, a love for others and genuine positive regard for their communities. Others, highly inactive and craving social contact, deeply distrust people or themselves. If we believe ourselves fairly treated and that others usually cooperate with us, if we imagine that they like us, then it's generally a safe bet that we are comfortable with them, too. Our inherent affection for others begets our good treatment.

- *Am I glad to be alive, regardless of bodily aches and pains, emotional ups and downs, and even serious disappointments?* A glad heart does not mean we are always "happy." Only a fool is happy all the time. If we eagerly start the day, if we are thankful for each day, if we are actively and intrinsically motivated to involve ourselves with people, projects and ideas "beyond" ourselves, we probably can manage frustration and productively engage our minds with meaningful purposes and goals. The more we appreciate life's gift, the more we can

---

*A friend calls herself pessimistic, says she always expects the worst. But her spirits and mood are generally high. She says, "The point is, if the worst *does* happen, I know I can cope with it. Maybe I only expect 'worsts' I know I can deal with. I never expect 'worsts' that would overwhelm me, and I move toward what I truly want."

assume that we are positive, lively people whom others enjoy. In addition to appraising our level of optimism, we may ask ourselves who taught us how and what to think? How sane and clear-minded were they? Did our teachers rest in solutions? Assessing the quality of the minds of those who raised us can help us understand ourselves.

WHY NEGATIVITY CAN HAUNT US

Without transcendent self-awareness, without properly managing our attention, we easily duplicate our childhood experiences in adulthood. For example, I once heard a drug addict say that the abusive intensity of her relationship with her parents is something she still craves today. She interpreted her parents' abuse as "natural," received stimulation from their negative attention, felt high excitement from having to live up to their impossibly brutal and inconsistent standards. Her vivid emotional memories and her electrically charged involvement with two significant adults imprinted so deeply on her awareness that she now feels unfulfilled if her love object is not cruel to her. "Nice," considerate, consistent men bore her. "There's nothing to anticipate, nothing to strive for. It's all so predictable." The fulfilling subtleties of warm, enduring love, true intimacy and commitment are impossible experiences for this woman—and will remain out of reach until she becomes willing to let go of the familiar, in her feeling life, and move into the unknown. In the same vein, she admits that drugs are important to her, "as much for the lows as for the highs they bring."

Perhaps in our national frenzy to stop the blight and misery caused by drugs we have overlooked one possibility: the mysterious appeal of misery. Some people find reward in suffering. Pain is their payoff. When we lack inner strength or the memory and habit of love, then the blues, negativity or hopelessness can seduce us with cunning, continual subtlety. If we fit this woman's profile, two helpful questions we can ask ourselves are: "Am I willing to be happy?" And "What would it cost me, what pain, what suffering and what feelings, memories or beliefs must I relinquish, to live a wholesome life?" Often our answers show us we must divorce certain familiar ideas or comfortable agonies that our parents (or significant others) taught us. In a sense, we married these ideas and feelings and our life reveals the offsprings of this coupling. The previous questions can stimulate our whole-sight, without which a productive life seems impossible. However, for those who realize they are emotionally locked into pain, therapy seems a prudent way out.*

HABITUAL NEGATIVITY

Several theories have been forwarded to explain habitual negativity. In the seventies, for example, we heard from the irreverent Dr. Eric Berne about personal programs. Berne's theory, within his framework of Transactional Analysis, was that powerful parental directives compel us to adopt what he termed "life-scripts." These dramas, comedies or soap operas are so thoroughly imprinted on a child's psyche that he/she emotionally owns a specific way of succeeding, or failing, in life. The script, Berne said, determines whether we win or lose at life, whom we marry, how many spouses, children, or friends we have, how healthy (or unhealthy) we are, how we live and die. Berne's teachings portrayed individual life in its dramatic unfolding much as if it were a fairy tale or myth.

Today, through best-sellers and popular talk shows on TV and radio, we delve even deeper into such notions, hear how dysfunctional family systems perpetuate themselves into succeeding generations. Family systems theory also puts forth the idea that there are roles or parts for every member: One child might inherit a hero's role. Another gets to play "victim." Whether we interpret our lives through our own insights, Transactional Analysis or family systems theory, we may realize that the underlying drama of our own life produces a predictable and patterned result. In large part, positive and negative mind-sets flow from our "script" or early family programs. These are habitual blueprints, clearly embedded in our consciousness. To change these, we must set in motion new and enhanced idea structures. These structures eventually alter our life's outcomes.

Whatever theory or lexicon we elect to explain our moods, it seems that cheer and gloom are often just habits of mind, however these were implanted in our psyches. Habits are encoded grooves or imprints in consciousness. These codes create automatic behaviors, predictable,

---

*Read, for example, David Shapiro's treatment of masochism, in which he underscores the rigidity, determination and special superiority some feel about their pain and how adroitly they work to protect this strategy.

reflexive responses. The longer we rely on them, the more we become hypnotically addicted to these behavior patterns, much as we can become addicted to chemicals.

Often we grow so accustomed to moods, sensations, a state of being—however negative—that these *feel* like friends. Then, as adults, we experience these feelings, moods or states as oddly pleasurable even when they are lethal. We can, however, extricate ourselves from the limitations of our bad habits. As noted, the success models of fully functioning creative adaptive people and the technique of Positive Structuring can help us fix new images in our minds. These bring equally new, enhanced results.

The ability to choose anew each day gives us our power to serve whatever seems good in us. Our choices are a way for us to direct ourselves toward the most desirable, constructive outcomes imaginable.

Those who consistently choose in favor of their good find themselves inextricably tied to certain benefits. They use their imagination to prosper and grow. They take one step at a time in their preferred direction. They learn from one experience. They solve problems responsibly and as best as they can. They search for ponies when coming upon a room filled with manure. They rest in solutions. Such persons innovate, are moved by the possibility of whatever is good and have faith—even in the face of visible opposition. As a result, they interpret the world, by and large, as a friendly, decent, hospitable place in which to live.

If we want to grow in similar directions, we must move gently and slowly toward outcomes we consciously want. Scores of people improvise their way out of seemingly dead-end problems by keeping their eye on their goals. Troubled couples do redesign marriage so that their bond and commitment continues. Others, for whom marriage ends, manage to live on happily without inordinate anger, guilt or struggle. We hear stories every day of people who despite physical handicaps live vigorously, perhaps even more fully than their neighbors. Men and women without previous training or formal degrees do find work in their chosen fields. Every day, people open their own small businesses—or join excellent companies. They work painstakingly to make their ventures a success. Sometimes people fail—even creatively adaptive people. They begin again, learning from their errors. Some take lesser jobs in desired professions or companies that are willing to give them a break. Students of all ages manage to stick to backbreaking study schedules or tedious, boring curriculums just to earn a degree that they then leverage into better opportunities.

No one rule or requirement fits all people. We must stop trying to laminate one successful person's exact formula onto our own lives. No one can tell another whether he or she should quit or stay put in this or that job or relationship. However, all of us *can* evaluate our personal choices and their outcomes, discerning whether or not the gestalt of our solutions brings us nearer to our life's true purposes. Once we spot our undesirable patterns, we can choose to change them for the better. Self-awareness helps free us from our automatic, knee-jerk responses. Starting another habit (e.g., adopting a more productive, positive mind) is a laudable first step.

Self-awakening of the sort I'm describing has always been largely out of reach for most of humanity. It is inconvenient, requires effort and means making a deep, thorough change of mind and heart. This kind of transformation separates us from the common stream of convention and day-to-day belonging: as we uproot our unconscious habits, we work hard to keep alert, to avoid mechanical responses. Sometimes this means we must separate ourselves from toxic people, however close they are to us in other respects.

As the 21st century nears, technological advances in what I'd call the science of mind-bending makes finding our true human power even more arduous. This is not because full awakening is any riskier than in decades past, but because the cultural overlay may now be stronger, subtler, more enticing and hypnotic than ever. For instance, what is now called "consumer engineering"—the contemporary use of psychology in print and electronic advertising, mass marketing and political campaigns—embodies the very enculturation process that has kept humankind in perceptual slumber since time began. It is estimated that in the late eighties industry alone spent $110 billion to market products, services and ideas for our consumption. We "eat" these pretty, instant image-packages just as surely as we eat fast foods. The faster and greater our consumption, the hungrier we get.

These seductive images, these idea campaigns, imprint our collective consciousness with the value of what we're sold. We believe what we are told much as "primitive" people believed the initiation rites, symbols, myths and cultural ideas of their time. However, today technological advances entertain us into ever deeper levels of hypnosis. These image-bites come at us faster and faster. They are fun, pretty, diverting and appetizing. Our enjoyment is part of the problem. Many, if not most, consumers hypnotically compare their bodies, faces, hairstyles, life-styles, relationships and financial and physical well-being to the ideals fed to them by magazines, radio and TV. Whatever people digest as successful, winning or healthy becomes true to them, molds their awareness and future choices, acts, thought patterns.

At the very least, we must understand how images, advertising imprints and the constant repetition of these ideas shape and structure our perceptions and reality. In fact, understanding isn't nearly enough. Most of us already have a sense of how pop culture forms and influences us. As we judge ourselves by media's perfected models, we must have some clue that we are being molded to an external rule and thereby forfeiting our autonomy.

More than understanding, we need at least minimal self-awareness about our own thought processes. Only this knowledge puts us in a watchful position to protect our minds. If we would be the authors of our beliefs, moods, values and life-purposes, an essential first step is to familiarize ourselves with our own thought-language. Usually, this starts with simple, consciousness-raising discussion or psychological help. In terms of very general awakening, an able therapist or some honest soul in an adult support group eventually asks us, "Why do you always act like such an idiot in all these situations?" Or, "When, as a child, did you think, behave or feel this way?" Such questions may shock us into noticing how our thoughts breed predictable results or how our patterned, habitual responses dominate us. But it takes much more than this to be fully aware of how our minds work. For this we need a simple mind, an open mind.

Creative adaptation implies a complete regeneration of being. This means we find ways and means to examine our own consciousness, become master of our mind's functions and gain nothing short of clear whole-sight.

POSITIVE STRUCTURING FOR GAINING WHOLE-SIGHT

A Sample Exercise

Positive Structuring is not a cure-all, not a psychological method. However, in conjunction with high-quality therapy, spiritual direction, or other professional counseling, the method seems rich with potential for thinking about our thinking. It is also full of lessons for our good future. Once on solid emotional footing and assured of our overall psychological health, we can create models and projects aimed to teach ourselves how to perceive the world more holistically and objectively.

Phase I: Exploration—Discovering "What"

Here again, we follow the general steps outlined previously. First, we decide what we want:

- What would it take for us to minimize our "social self"?
- Why do we aim for this—what, to us, does whole-sight mean and what do we think is our true objective?
- Does a narrow, particular area of our life need overhauling? Or are we hoping to move beyond a specific solution into a way of life that is actively creative, spontaneous, fresh, etc.? What would it take for us to achieve this second aim, and who do we know that has reached this? What teachers might we find (e.g., in books, lectures, workshops, etc.) to help us see ourselves clearly, then gain skills of the sort we want?
- When are we most creatively adaptive? What mental processes, environmental conditions, ideas, stimulate our finest thinking?
- Who made up our life's rules? Whose life are we living? How do we know we are not just running in a different direction (i.e., opposite) while continuing to avoid, polarize and fragment experience?
- What do we *believe* stands in the way of our joy, prosperity, full-functioning and active, creative problem-solving?
- Would we be willing to change our minds, give up our limiting beliefs, if this was a way to the life we want?
- To whom might we turn for objective feedback on these matters? How competent are they?

We must shy away from two extreme camps: one instills in us the belief that we can never achieve whole-sight. The other tells us it's a snap, that in this or that weekend workshop we instantly can find our way. The truth lives somewhere in between.

First, we can lift our minds, clarify our goals and gain transcendent, directive insights simply by speaking to ourselves during this exploratory phase in a respectful, meditative manner. For example, many people report that when they sit quietly and comfortably before going to sleep at night, and objectively ask themselves what is needed to feel better or to accomplish something, their dreams answer these questions. Or, early the next morning (if dreams have been unproductive), they might sit meditatively with pen and paper in hand, waiting, in this silence, for answers. When we expect responses from ourselves, we receive them. This waiting is an art, not a science; each person must find what works best.

Sometimes answers arrive immediately. When they don't, we just go about our day as usual, with an added air of positive expectancy that says the direction we seek will somehow be forthcoming. There is no need to mystify the matter or to hold our thought in a certain fixed way. News articles or reports, books, discussions with friends, a chance remark spoken by a complete stranger—any of these become realistic sources for the exact bit of knowledge we want. We will come upon what we require to pinpoint what we need in order to grow healthier. We do not look for signs, nor stupefy ourselves into trances. We merely increase our subjective acuity, become receptive to nonconscious data already present in, or around, us, available for use.

Phase II: Research—Plumbing the Depths

After clarifying our specific needs, we then try to enter fully into the spirit of these. If we hope for greater mindfulness, we can read about how humans adopt their belief systems, values, their patterns of perception. Or, we might study transformational thinkers whom we admire. It is important to find models with whom we feel some sympathetic resonance. Often such individuals—those who espouse the possibilities of enlightenment or self-actualization—strike others as people who deny the ugly realities of the world as well as their own dark side. If time goes by and we can't locate anyone to observe in our sphere of friends or community, or if we resist the exercise entirely due to procrastination, inordinate fear, prejudice—then we'd best return to the first stage of this practice and ask ourselves if we really want the goal of greater objectivity. What it would cost us to give up our smaller, culturally based self? When we spot our resistance, this, too, is a sensible time to consider therapy, spiritual direction or a trusted friend's objectivity to augment our own, quite possibly biased, thinking.

Phase III: Solution Architecture—Creating a Model

Let us say we find our way into the spirit of greater objectivity, locate and observe a few admired role models and have built a composite picture of the skills, values, worldview and behaviors we want. Perhaps we have also gone to a few reputable workshops or adult education courses on the topic. We feel committed to continue. Now we are ready to create some low-risk, physical or experiential models.

This third stage suggests its own levels or hierarchy of complexity. Initially, we can simply write a short story, a play or a poem, describing ourselves as the key character around whom the plot then revolves. In itself, this written exercise greatly enhances whatever visualization we may do. Writing fiction in this way forces us to become specific, moves our thinking to the particulars of what originally may be only a hazy notion of whole-seeing. As we immerse ourselves in descriptive language and images, as we adopt the feelings or sensory details surrounding our assignment, we find ourselves gradually raising our consciousness about what we want. For instance, the early models make the goal seem possible, not so out of reach. Our observations, notes, meditations and writings are positive representations, or shadows, of the thing to come. These link us to other people, attitudes, books or opportunities.

We now seek additional information because our minds have opened up. Even our reason, our logical process, gets brighter as a result of this slow, but focused, study. The words we use in our writings can easily open up new realities; now we choose our vocabulary carefully and with as much vivid feeling or accuracy as we can muster. If we write in concrete, clear word pictures, our daydreams and visualizations are enhanced. Indirectly, in our own time and way, certainly at our own pace, we blend these language study-models into daily life and this merger prepares our awareness still further for receipt of what we want. We should not forget that regressive tendencies exist in all of us; to take three small steps forward may provoke a self-protective reaction of taking two steps—or more—back. Perhaps this is why Positive Structuring works—its steps forward are so innocent that fear-laden reactions are less likely to result.

LENGTHIER POSITIVE STRUCTURING TASKS

A later Positive Structuring exercise for gaining objectivity might be to adopt any one of a number of Buddhist disciplines or ways of seeing. Thus, we rid ourselves gradually of the tendency to project our biases—say, perfectionism—onto others. An inclination to judge harshly, a tendency to blame or see only flaws or undesirable elements (rather than to accept people and things for what they are) are signs of a double mind. This, too, may be corrected by disciplining our attention, as a case in point shows:

A bright young manager complained about his supervisor. This manager was supercritical, and I proposed he try the following exercise: For one or two weeks, during his normal business day, he was to describe (mentally) every material object that he noticed by defining what it was and what it wasn't. For instance, when entering his office, he might say to himself, "This oak desk is made of laminated wood. On the other hand, this floor is pegged, and polished, unlike that wall, which is wallpapered." He was not to editorialize his subjective preferences, not to say, "I like my floor at home better than this; I hate this cheap desk; Who found that tasteless wallpaper?" His narrative was merely a help to distinguish one thing from another, and identify the distinctive class of each thing he saw.

After that (for about two or three more weeks), he was to expand this ongoing objective commentary to include people in his differentiating activity. He might ask himself while at lunch with a group of coworkers what makes each person unique: "Hank is not like Mary," "Mary is unlike Joe." "Both Hank and Joe are tall and skinny, but Herman is stocky and unlike Roberta, who is round, full and not muscular." In a month, we spoke again. I asked him for his update on this project. He admitted that at first, for about two days, the exercise had been tedious and boring. He'd been angry at himself for agreeing to try it. Perhaps trusting some certainty or hopefulness on my part, he plodded on. Soon he found his perception drastically altered. He was releasing old negativities:

I gradually gained what can only be called "clarity." I noticed crisp distinctions, or lines, around things and people—they became wholly themselves, unlike anything or anyone else. I felt they were perfect in their imperfections.

I found myself laughing as the hilarity of this way of seeing struck me—here I'd spent some twenty-five years judging myself, everyone else, picking away at things, wishing everything was something it wasn't, and all the time everything and everyone was perfect in a distinctive, particular way. What a shock.

If we can sustain our interest beyond this level, then we are ready to create something physical. Again, our prototype must satisfy our goal's requirement; for instance, help us eliminate a tendency to expect the worst, harp critically or see things as hopeless. Our study model should help us cultivate a positive, objective, yet practical outlook. At no time are we straining for a mindless "Don't worry, be happy" mentality that buries our intelligence and discernment under simplistic, reality-denying and largely phony bliss. Unless we think of ourselves as cartoon characters, the dark side and strangeness of life are natural companions to the light. These can be used to enrich and empower us.

Suppose, following the example provided in our previous chapter, we decide to amplify our pessimistic tendency as a way of gaining objectivity and thus control. We might purposely put ourselves in low-risk, negative situations—possibly even create playful, odious replicas of our life's melodrama—in order to watch ourselves be critical. Professional athletes who review videos of their mishaps do so in order to avoid repeating them. Or we could design a concrete study model of optimism, say, in our garage or garden. One master gardener gives us an example of what this could be like. Obviously a positive thinker, he said he had high faith in the blossoming power inherent in seeds. "I don't believe in regionalist thinking—I never read seed packets. I just plant whatever flowers I like and expect them to flourish. Most of them do." In this way, we, too, could plant flowers that don't normally grow in our geographic region as a symbolic gesture of faith and optimism.

If we hate getting up in the morning, we can set our alarm one hour early and then watch ourselves struggle to leave our warm bed. If we detest exercise, we can take ourselves out for a brisk walk and observe our tendency to resist, return home sooner than planned, avoid the whole experience. A woman who had unsuccessfully tried to exercise for years because she gave in to her sense of fatigue and physical limitation began to "live in the spirit of health and fitness," as she put it. "When I went for walks, I simply used my imagination to enter the spirit of energized health. My body complained about this—lungs said, 'I need more air,' legs said, 'We hurt.' In a responsible way, I just kept living in the spirit of health, kept that image and feeling alive in my mind's eye while walking up steeper hills and longer terrains. Lo and behold, now it's easy for me to take those hills and those long outings." The idea is not to go against ourselves in any rough, insensitive way, but merely to notice our reactions, feel what we feel, hear what we tell ourselves when we think we "can't" do something. In time, we realize that gaining optimism or the energy to get up early in the morning or take walks are simply neutral goals. Our minds embellish these objectives and experiences with emotion and positive/negative interpretations.

Soon we can expect ourselves to draw productive insights and outcomes from these negative simulations. As other examples, we can join a neighborhood theater group to have an experience of acting "as if" we were pessimists. Or we could reverse this, play the eternal optimist—observe ourselves as Polyanna types. We can take up a sport that we now dislike, unemotionally attending to our predictable reactions during all the early learning stages, and finally practicing with as much detachment as we can muster. We might enroll in a square dance class to see how we resolve the awkwardness of that activity. We stick with it. We teach our minds to perceive matters without such emotional charge, then in the way we prefer.

Our mind is our possession. We do not belong to it. We can command it to think in this or that way, but not if we can't "lift up," out of our thoughts, long enough to see our mind's workings. Once we realize that we alone are responsible for our thoughts, we can tell our mind what and how to think. Now we discover that positivity and negativity are simply choices. This insight means we can play with reality whenever we choose. We can create solution architectures, structure this (or any other) truth into our perceptual system. A long-time housekeeper in Mary Baker Eddy's Chestnut Hill home described the way Mrs. Eddy's exactness and orderliness began in small daily routines and practices. Eddy, the discoverer and founder of Christian Science, believed that the human mind reflects Mind (another word for God in Christian Science). She taught the members of her household to demonstrate perfection in the tiniest details:

Even the different lengths of pins had their respective corners in her pincushion and she took out the pin she needed, without taking out and putting back the different lengths. No one would have thought of changing a pin in her pincushion. Mrs. Eddy believed that if one's thought was not orderly and exact in the things that make up present consciousness, that same thought would not be exact enough to give a treatment or use an exact science. (Wilcox, 1979, p. 201)

We may deride such precision or laugh at it as excessive until we grow in wisdom about our own consciousness, our ground of being. Then we understand that however *we* interpret it, the slightest physical act has enormously far-reaching ramifications in our consciousness. A mere pin can represent the way to an enhanced life if we are creatively adaptive enough to find the logical, symbolic connections.

Any of us can design study models that transform life for the better and thereby gain a brighter future. We might make dirt paths into beautiful, flowery ones; we could turn rusty, discarded objects into polished, valued treasures. We might renovate an old attic or building or create a new blouse or work shirt out of rags and remnants. At work we could resurrect a hopeless, turned-off customer, try to renew old, lost ties and loyalties. Ideally, since one aim under discussion is to reinterpret negative circumstances more positively, we can learn to see the challenge in problems, instead of only the tough, unappealing work or misery. We could even turn a manure heap into a community compost, and—by helping our neighbors and friends while also helping ourselves—we might finally realize the purpose of all this play.

IN SUM: INVENTING YOUR BRIGHTER FUTURE

Positive Structuring is our forum for teaching ourselves how to invent and achieve a brighter future. It lets us play with reality, monitor and "create" thought, design physical and experiential models, hone our perceptual and practical, real-world skills. A Positive Structuring study model is our low-risk lab, our engaging, hopefully amusing simulation of what we want to be, do or have. Positive Structuring holds the premise that our life outcomes are a byproduct of the patterns we establish in consciousness. As we identify and then enter the spirit of the things we want, we begin to construct channels of clarity about such patterns as well as ideas, perception and activity that then return to us expanded, totally new opportunities for receiving what we want.

In effect, we use the appropriate study models to imprint our consciousness with the qualities and characteristics of our goals, even though we are working on lesser levels and with much smaller, seemingly unrelated projects. Positive Structuring is a technique for building metaphorical mental models that eventually generate countless insights about how we might meet our long-range objectives and find our good. The metaphysician Ralph Waldo Trine wrote:

> Every thought you entertain is a thought that goes out and every thought comes back laden with its kind. . . . You are then continually building [these qualities and thoughts] into both your mental and your physical life, and so your life is enriched by [this influence]. (Trine, 1897, pp. 94–95)

And this is exactly why Positive Structuring works.

If our models are too aggressive, if we are overly ambitious, if we undermine ourselves in any way by grandiose exaggerations of the technique, we have failed to grasp the gentle, meditative, easygoing nature of this method, a method that simply asks us to build up thoughts, then construct metaphors, of our desires. If we are too strident we must take responsibility for our unbridled tendency to do ourselves in. Ownership of this sort is critical here, since excessive aggression can be a sign that our old-fashioned mind still rules us. The too rough or warlike mind is what must change.

Through Positive Structuring models we may start to possess our minds in a way that can, should we persevere, bring enlightenment. In time, we "see" our thoughts; they bubble up in front of us exactly like translucent balls. We begin to hear our customary inner dialogue, realize the truth in the proverb that "As a man thinketh, so is he." By degrees we realize that we can be or accomplish what our thoughts told us was difficult, troublesome or even impossible. As we invent the ways and means to immerse ourselves in solutions, we learn about and trust our higher mind's powers. Dwelling on and playing with solutions, we leave behind our old mind, with its limited scenarios and small, egocentric lack of vision. In this way personal characteristics, like the ones described in this book, or more visible factors—like finances or relationships or even health—are improved.

We must also remember that a book can only tell us about a subject. It is our reflection and our own experiential understanding of the matter that helps us apply, or put any truths to use. For this reason, it is outside the scope and intent of this book to list every eventuality or every possible Positive Structuring model. Even if I wanted to draw up such a list, since there are infinite variables, this would be impossible.

The study model is the zero point from which, in playful, thoughtful innocence, we can learn how fundamentally able we are. The models show us how we ourselves shape our thinking; these also teach us that consciousness speaks its own delicate, reality-shaping language. Gradually, we "hear" our interior, quite-wordless voice, commune with that silent, sacred void. We decipher the nature of this energy or power. As we learn to listen inwardly, as we guide and impress desirable images or motifs on our own consciousness (through its unique dialects of thought, faith, feeling and playful, concentrated, inventive action), as we see ourselves participating in and improving our external world, we really play. We make our outer world a reflection of our inmost being and create order, beauty, sanity and distinctiveness where previously there was none. The wonderful truth is that wherever we are right now, we can start.

The models help us use today to dream up small, manageable ways to fix new patterns in consciousness; to be, do and have what we want. In fact, the more we link ourselves to our own inner core of thought, the fewer things have hold on us, the less we want. Here, in this silent core, we see that material things can never give us anything of lasting value, but that an illuminated mind makes for a truly bright future. Rainer Maria Rilke's words, "If your [life] seems poor . . . blame yourself; admit to yourself that you are not enough of a poet to call forth its riches," sums this up. The instant we grasp this truth, our growth toward enlightened functioning begins.

Ordinary psychology, that which stresses only problems or our pitiful past and endless struggles, may well define creativity as a neurotic impulse. But this outlook seems passé. It weakens us, keeps us childishly dependent on our old mind, on other people's labels, interpretations of us or on the world's viewpoint. That point of view assumes that externals create the individual while he or she, passive and helpless, tries in vain to conform to what is expected. On the other hand, as we meet and learn to trust our naturally inventive, unitive core—our highest universal self—we find the very power needed to have the life we truly want. Then we can rest in solutions. We find ways to manage our attention and shape ourselves, outgrowing the impoverished limits of our small mind over time.

I repeat: illumined, widened minds are ever with us. These have always been around. If we look to our finest artists, poets, dancers or cutting-edge scientists; if we study gifted teachers, inventors, salesmen, statesmen, entrepreneurs or peacemakers; if we observere any joyful, inspired, life-filled and loving persons, we find individuals with psychic health shining from them like warm, bright light. Finding them, we simultaneously find 21st-century minds. But first, before locating such models, we may need to train ourselves to see more generously. After all, it takes one to know one.

A magnanimous mind is a power unto itself and would seem the point of much, if not all, that has been outlined thus far. To me, E. E. Cummings had a 21st-century mind. We see it evidenced in his description of his mother. Here again, we can note the quality of his thought in his attention and in his language:

I have the honor [of being] a true heroine's son . . . [Her religion] was an integral part of herself, she expressed it as she breathed and as she smiled. The two indispensable factors in life, my mother always maintained, were "health and a sense of humor." And although her health eventually failed her, she kept her sense of humor to the beginning. (Cummings, 1953, p. 12)

No doubt many readers will automatically ask, "What if we weren't so fortunate as to have been a hero's or heroine's offspring?" What if we were not raised by parents who—like Eudora Welty's—whistled their greetings lovingly to each other every morning? What if our parents were abusive or thoroughly toxic? What if they lacked healthy spirituality, and their despair flowed from them as did their ill humor? What if, because of this, we know our minds have a self-protective wall or a stingy side, cause us to view ourselves, others and the world as unattractive, wanting and in pain? Well, then, we can join the club. For this is almost everyone's condition. Surely the bulk of humankind lacks secure, loving childhood memories. No matter. For here we find our natural first objective for Positive Structuring's initial models.

We can begin right here to create the metaphorical mental models that we want, can start today to imagine how we might teach ourselves to Positively Structure good, emotionally and spiritually whole parents in our mind. Or we can learn to plant, in consciousness, the seeds of anything else we feel we need and want.

If we can't fathom the simplicity of all of this, if we can't quite grasp the full, rich power and potential of this metaphorical method, we needn't worry. Then we just go slower, begin at the beginning, take smaller, more reflective bites of what has been presented. We chew up each morsel thoroughly before foraging greedily ahead. This, too, builds a discipline of mind that will, in the long run, pay off, help us grow. In time, with steady practice and modest, prudent starts, we can construct the exact mental models we need. No matter where we begin on all of this, the work automatically enriches us because such thinking cultivates our mind's inventive functions, produces greater creative adaptivity.

Through proper, disciplined reflection, and with the experience of gently structured, metaphorical play, we open up perception's doors. These clearings reveal one important aim of life: to learn how to guide the dynamic, unlimited energies of our own mind into beautiful, productive thought structures—the most elevated and aesthetic we can discover. In time we figure out "how" to translate these constructions into practical, real-world expressions. In other words, we learn how to build a worthwhile life. Predictably, we realize that not only Positive Structuring models, but also external circumstances and even memories, are, at root, just constructions and artifacts of mind—plays and patterns of awareness that at some level—however high, low or hidden—are for our enjoyment, learning and, ultimately, our overcoming. When we see this, we see the perfect.

REFERENCES

Arasteh, Reza A. 1965. *Final Integration in the Adult Personality*. New York: E. J. Brill.

Arieti, Silvano. 1976. *Creativity: The Magic Synthesis*. New York: Basic Books.

Bancroft, Anne. 1979. *Zen*. New York: Thames and Hudson.

Bennett, Amanda. 1988. "Survivors on Corporate Staffs Yearn for the Security of Yore," *Wall Street Journal*, Eastern edition, May 4.

Blyth, R. H. 1976. *Games Zen Masters Play*. New York: New American Library.

Bolin, Jean. 1979. *The Tao of Psychology*. New York: Harper & Row.

Bolles, Richard N. 1972. *What Color Is Your Parachute?* Berkeley, Calif.: Ten Speed Press.

Brown, Christy. 1989. *My Left Foot*. London: Mandarin Books.

Buber, Martin. 1985. *Ecstatic Confessions*, ed. Paul Medes-Slohr. New York: Harper & Row.

Buechner, Frederick. 1975. *Wishful Thinking*. New York: Harper & Row.

Cross, Robert. 1989. "Finding Liberty in Less," *Houston Chronicle*, December 28.

Cummings, E. E. 1953. *Six Nonlectures*. Cambridge, Mass.: Harvard University Press.

——. 1959. *100 Selected Poems*. New York: Grove Press.

Delayne, Gayle. 1979. *Living Your Dreams*. New York: Harper & Row.

Dillard, Annie. 1989. *The Writing Life*. New York: Harper & Row.

Eikerenkotter, Frederick. *Science of Living Study Guide*. Science of Living Publications, Box 130, Brooklyn, MA 02146.

Feldenkrais, Moshe. 1981. *The Elusive Obvious*. Cupertino, Calif.: Meta Publications.

Fisher, Roger, and William Ury. 1987. *Getting to Yes*. Middlesex, England: Penguin Books.

Gallwey, Timothy. 1974. *Inner Game of Tennis*. New York: Random House.

Gardner, John. 1969. *No Easy Victories.* New York: Harper Colophon.

Gardner, John. 1985. *On Becoming a Novelist.* New York: Harper & Row Perennial Library.

Geldof, Bob. 1986. *Is That All There Is?* New York: Ballantine.

Goldberg, Philip. 1983. *The Intuitive Edge.* Los Angeles: Jeremy P. Tarcher.

Gundin, Robert. 1982. *Time and the Art of Living.* New York: Harper & Row.

Hayes, Charles D. 1989. *Self-University.* Wasilla, Alaska: Autodidactic Press.

Ho Chi Minh. 1971. *The Prison Diary of Ho Chi Minh.* New York: Bantam.

Horney, Karen. 1950. *Neurosis and Human Growth.* New York: W. W. Norton.

John-Steiner, Vera. 1987. *Notebooks of the Mind.* New York: Harper & Row.

Jung, Carl. 1953. *Psychological Reflections,* ed. Jolandi Jacobi, Bollingen Series XXXI. Princeton, NJ: Princeton University Press.

————. 1954. *The Development of Personality,* trans. R. F. C. Hull. New York: Bollingen.

————. 1957. *The Undiscovered Self.* Boston: Little, Brown.

————. 1964. *Man and His Symbols.* New York: Dell, 1964.

King, Serge. 1891. *Imagineering.* Wheaton, Ill.: Quest Books.

Lakoff, George, and Mark Johnson. 1980. *Metaphors We Live By.* Chicago: University of Chicago Press.

Leonard, George. 1975. *The Ultimate Athlete.* New York: Viking Press.

Lichtenstein, BenYamin M. 1990. "Praxsyma: Tools for Creating a Just Society," *Proceeds, International Society of Systems Sciences,* 34th Annual Meeting, Portland, Oregon.

Ludlum, Robert. 1982. *The Road to Gandolfo.* New York: Bantam Books.

May, Rollo. 1975. *The Courage to Create.* New York: Bantam.

Merton, Thomas. 1961. *The New Man.* New York: Farrar, Strauss & Giroux.

Morse, John, ed. 1972. *Ben Shahn.* New York: Praeger Publishers.

Moyers, Bill. 1990. *Public Mind,* PBS TV, January 20.

Naisbitt, John. 1990. "Trend Letter." *Global Network,* Vol. 9, No. 10 (May 10).

Orr, Leonard. 1977. *Rebirthing in a New Age.* Millbrae, Calif.: Celestial Arts.

Papert, Seymour. 1980. *Mindstorms.* New York: Basic Boosk.

Pines, Maya. 1980. "Psychological Hardiness," *Psychology Today*, Vol. 14, No. 7, pp. 39–40.

———. 1984. "Resilient Children," *American Educator*, Vol. 8, No. 3 (Fall), pp. 34–37.

Ponder, Catherine. 1971. *Open Your Mind to Prosperity*. Unity Village, Mo.: Unity School.

Powell, James N. 1982. *Tao of Symbols*. New York: Quill Books.

Progoff, Ira. 1985. *Intensive Journal Workshop*. New York: Dialogue House Library.

Rheingold, Howard. 1988. *They Have a Word for It*. Los Angeles: Jeremy P. Tarcher.

Robbins, Anthony. 1987. *Unlimited Power*. New York: Fawcett Columbine.

Salinger, J. D. 1953. *Nine Stories*. New York: Bantam Books.

Shapiro, David. 1981. *Autonomy and Rigid Character*. New York: Harper Torchbooks.

Sinetar, Marsha. 1980. "Management in the New Age: An Exploration of Changing Work Values," *Personnel Journal*, Vol. 59, No. 9 (September), pp. 749–755.

———. 1986. *Ordinary People as Monks and Mystics*. Mahwah, N.J.: Paulist Press.

———. 1987. *Do What You Love, the Money Will Follow*. Mahwah, N.J.: Paulist Press.

———. 1988. *Elegant Choices, Healing Choices*. Mahwah, N.J.: Paulist Press.

———. 1990. *Living Happily Ever After*. New York: Villard Books.

Stoddard, Alexandra. 1986. *Living a Beautiful Life*. New York: Avon Books.

Sutherland, Audrey. 1986. *Paddling My Own Canoe*. Honolulu: University of Hawaii Press.

Toffler, Alvin. 1970. *Future Shock*. New York: Bantam Books.

Trine, Ralph Waldo. 1897. *In Tune with the Infinite*. New York: Thomas Y. Crowell.

Troward, Thomas. 1909. *The Dore Lectures*. New York: Dodd, Mead.

Tyler, Anne. 1982. *Dinner at the Homesick Restaurant*. New York: Berkley Books.

Ueland, Brenda. 1987. *If You Want to Write*. St. Paul Minn.: Graywolf Press.

Welty, Eudora. 1983. *One Writer's Beginnings*. New York: Warner Books.

Wilcox, Martha. 1979. *We Knew Mary Baker Eddy.* Boston: Christian Science Publication Society.

Winter, Nina. 1978. *Interviews with the Muse.* Berkeley, CA: Moon Books.

Yamamoto, Kaoru. 1972. *The Child and His Image.* Boston: Houghton Mifflin.

ABOUT THE AUTHOR

MARSHA SINETAR has long been immersed in the study of creatively gifted, spiritually emerging adults. An educator and author, she began her professional career as a teacher, then moved rapidly through the ranks of public education as a principal, curriculum specialist, and university lecturer. In 1980 she founded her own private human resource advisory firm in Santa Rosa, California. Her six previously published books are used worldwide in a growing number of diverse professional settings—in colleges, therapeutic sessions, and spiritual direction programs. Marsha Sinetar lives and works at her home in Northern California, "as quietly and simply as possible," among the coastal redwoods.